Is the Atheist My Neighbor?

Is the Atheist My Neighbor?

Rethinking Christian Attitudes toward Atheism

RANDAL RAUSER

CASCADE *Books* · Eugene, Oregon

IS THE ATHEIST MY NEIGHBOR?
Rethinking Christian Attitudes toward Atheism

Cascade Books
An Imprint of Wipf and Stock Publishers
199 W. 8th Ave., Suite 3
Eugene, OR 97401

www.wipfandstock.com

ISBN 13: 978-1-4982-1716-3

Cataloging-in-Publication data:

Rauser, Randal D.

    Is the atheist my neighbor? : rethinking Christian attitudes toward atheism / Randal Rauser.

    xii + 104 p.; 23 cm—Includes bibliographical references.

    ISBN 13: 978-1-4982-1716-3

    1. Christianity and atheism—Miscellanea. 2. Atheism—Miscellanea. 3. Dialogue—Religious aspects—Christianity. I. Lowder, Jeffery Jay. II. Title.

BR128.A8 R387 2015

Manufactured in the USA.

This book is for all those who ever hoped God exists.

Thesis:

Contends Rebellion Thesis is

(one knows God exists but is rebelling against God
due to hatred, desire for immoral beh, lack of want, etc.)

- misunderstood
- misused by Christians to abuse atheist neighbors
'fool' - doesn't really mean one who doesn't believe in God / atheist
but rather extends to all people -
who know God exists but live otherwise (all in rebellion)

- But Ⓐ, he contends, disbelieve for
philosophical, experiential, intellectual reasons,
not out of rebellion.

- acknowledges Ⓐ who admit their lack of desire
for God (eg Hitchens, Nagel), but also dismisses the
Rebellion thesis in those cases.

RⓇ
Recommends we as Christians stop beating atheists & RT stick,
stop falsely assuming / stereotyping / negatively characterizing
atheists — just building walls.
Instead win Ⓐ through building bridges, engaging,
being generously hospitable.

con: → Overreaching analysis - rejecting RT in all cases just
because it has been abused / misused.
throwing out baby & bathwater.

- RT, as admitted by RⓇ, is a part of our resistance to God -
atheists and nonatheists - so to say it is not part
of the picture is being disingenuous, naive, +
unfaithful to Scriptural teaching —

dismisses ingaging both
sides of his notion.
· all are guilty of Reb.
· Ⓐ are not

(We all stand guilty)

pro - caution not to overuse / misuse / abuse. Ⓔ Practice hospitality.

There is a difference b/t use of rhetoric
and a dismissal / giving of truth.

Table of Contents

Acknowledgments ix

Introduction: The Parable of the Good ~~Samaritan~~ Atheist xi

1 The pastor said, "Atheists are brain dead" 1

2 April 1st is Atheist Day: Christian attitudes toward atheists 10

3 Does the Bible say atheists are fools? 32

4 Do atheists have an axe to grind? 47

5 What about the atheists who say they don't want there to be a God? 65

6 The atheist as neighbor 85

Bibliography 99

Acknowledgments

First of all, I'd like to thank my family. I've already thanked them several times in other books and at this point I'm starting to run out of ideas so I asked them what they'd like me to say. This is what my daughter suggested I write: "Thanks to my super amazing swimmer daughter." So that's done. As for my wife, she humbly advised me to thank my "dog caretaker" (we have two demanding lapdogs). As for my professional relationships, thanks go to my editor Robin Parry and the helpful staff at Wipf and Stock for enthusiastically embracing this project. [Robin adds, "You didn't ask me what I wanted you to say! Excuse me while I weep."] Finally, special thanks go to Jeff Lowder for agreeing to be interviewed in the book and providing such a fine example of an atheistic (and naturalistic) worldview in the process. Thanks Jeff, the book is much richer with your contribution!

Introduction

The Parable of the Good ~~Samaritan~~ Atheist

One day at a Starbucks in southern California an expert in the Bible stood up to test Jesus. "Teacher," he asked while sipping his Americano, "what must I do to inherit eternal life?"

"What is written in the Law?" Jesus replied. "How do you read it?"

He answered, "'Love the Lord your God with all your heart and with all your soul and with all your strength and with all your mind'; and, 'Love your neighbor as yourself.'"

"You have answered correctly," Jesus replied. "Do this and you will live."

But he wanted to justify himself, so he asked Jesus, "And who is my neighbor?"

In reply, Jesus said:

"A man was driving from San Diego to Los Angeles when he was carjacked by robbers. They stripped him of his clothes, beat him and went away, leaving him half dead. A Christian pastor from a mega church in San Bernardino happened to be going down the interstate, and when he saw the man, he passed by on the other side. A little while later a famous theologian from a seminary in La Mirada was driving by when he came to the place and saw him. But he was late for class and so he passed by on the other side.

A short while after this a famous atheist was on his way to a skeptics' convention at UCLA. As he drove along in his Toyota Prius (it's the one with a Darwin fish sticker on the bumper) he came to where the man was; and when he saw him, he took pity on him. He pulled onto the shoulder of the road, went out, and administered first aid. Then he put the man in the back seat of the Prius and brought him to a local hospital. The hospital demanded to see the man's health insurance. 'I don't know that he has any,' said the atheist. So he pulled out his credit card. 'Look after him,' he said, 'and you can charge any necessary expenses on my card.'

"Which of these three do you think was a neighbor to the man who fell into the hands of robbers?"

The expert in the Bible replied, "The one who had mercy on him."

Jesus told him, "Go and do likewise."

You might possibly find a good Samaritan if you looked really hard. But a good *atheist*?

1

The pastor said, "Atheists are brain dead"

Pastor John Hagee *really* doesn't like atheists. Whenever the topic of the godless comes up in his sermons, Hagee lets them have it with both barrels blazing. And it isn't hard to see why: attacking atheists seems to be a sure way to rile up the crowd, for his harangues regularly invite raucous applause and even standing ovations from the boisterous congregation. Consider this fiery excerpt that Hagee recently delivered from the pulpit:

> The Bible says, "The fool has said in his heart there is no God." Atheists say there is no God. Let me tell you that atheism has never painted a masterpiece. Atheism has never dispelled fear. Atheism has never healed a disease. Faith in God has, but not atheism. Atheism has never given anyone peace of mind. Atheism has never dried a tear. Atheism has never given an intellectual answer to the creation. Atheism is bankrupt and empty. It's brain dead![1]

Take note: Those with weaker constitutions can leave their seeker sensitivity at the door. Hagee calls it like he sees it, and if he sees atheists to be brain dead fools, he'll be more than willing to speak his mind.

In case you think that Hagee was just having a bad day, on another occasion he offered the following blunt advice to any atheists he may have offended: "To the atheist watching this telecast, if our belief in God offends you . . . *move!* There are planes leaving every hour on the hour going every

---

1. Right Wing Watch. "Atheism Has Never Healed a Disease."

place on planet earth. *Get on one.* We don't want you and we won't miss you, I promise you."[2]

Yikes.

When you think about it, this is an extraordinary picture: one of America's leading pastors denouncing a significant portion of the American population—a group that includes a broad cross-section of society—as *brain dead.* And then to add insult to injury, he advises them that if they don't like his diagnosis, they can get out of the country because they're not wanted and they won't be missed.

I'm not saying that Christians need to buy wholesale into the seeker sensitive movement, but isn't this a bit much?

And just so we're clear, Hagee and his church (Cornerstone Church in San Antonio, Texas) are not a fringe group like Westboro Baptist, that club of forty misanthropes in Topeka, Kansas who picket everything on behalf of the wrath of God. Cornerstone Church is in the mainstream of North American Christianity with more than 20,000 people in weekly attendance. Hagee's sermons are televised around the world, he regularly appears on Christian and secular media outlets, and several of his books have topped the *New York Times* Bestseller list. So his opinions matter, and if Hagee thinks atheists are "brain dead," you can bet other Christians do as well.

God's not dead. But the atheist professor is

Okay, so Hagee's clearly a mover and a shaker and he believes atheists are basically dullards. But could it be that his views on atheism are idiosyncratic, and thus not representative of mainstream Christian views?

That is certainly possible. However, the evidence instead suggests to the contrary that Hagee's hostility is representative of the conservative Christian mainstream. Just consider the 2014 film *God's Not Dead*, which centers on the intellectual duel between a young Christian student and his atheistic philosophy professor. Made on a shoestring budget of two million dollars, the movie went on to gross over sixty million dollars at the box office. And its amazing run of success has continued on DVD: as of late October, 2014 (a mere three months after its release to DVD) it had garnered over 3,000 reviews on Amazon.com with an impressive average 4 ½ stars rating. Bottom line: this movie was a formidable mainstream box

2. Right Wing Watch. "Hagee Tells Atheists To Leave the Country b/c They Are Not Wanted & Won't Be Missed."

office success which was buoyed to those heights by legions of Christian movie goers. So how does it depict atheists?

The picture isn't pretty. The story focuses on the confrontation between atheist philosophy professor Jeffery Radisson (Kevin Sorbo) and a young evangelical Christian student named Josh Wheaton (Shane Harper). On the first day of class Professor Radisson directs all the students to write "God is dead," Nietzsche's infamous declaration, on a sheet of paper. Only one student, young Josh, refuses to do so. Radisson is outraged at the young man's intransigence. And so as punishment he demands that Josh defend God's existence in front of the class over the next three sessions.

Josh takes up the challenge. Despite the fact that he is merely a freshman facing the overwhelming first semester of university, he still manages to prepare and deliver a sequence of presentations defending God's existence (replete with animation and graphics) which is so sophisticated and polished that it could impress any TED talk audience. There is no question about who wins *this* debate. At the end of Josh's three lectures, his fellow students all stand, one after another, to declare him the clear winner over Professor Radisson. Although all eighty of these students had declared that "God is dead" only three classes before, now every one of them apparently believes God exists.[3]

The starkness of the outcome raises an important question: if the evidence for God is really this overwhelming, then why is Professor Radisson an atheist in the first place? That question is answered at one point in the film when Radisson dramatically reveals that he is deeply angry at God for allowing his mother to die when he was twelve. In other words, Radisson's unbelief is not an *intellectual* position. Instead, his sophisticated philosophical atheism is really just a veneer for a deeply-seated anger at God. The film provides a particularly insightful glimpse into that rebellious character when Radisson meets Josh in the hallway and snarls, "There *is* a god, and *I'm him*." It would seem that Radisson needs to be in charge. No wonder he's got a God problem.

Near the end of the movie seemingly everybody in town converges on a Newsboys concert during which the lead singer, Michael Tait, instructs the audience to send a text declaring "God's not dead" to all their phone contacts in honor of the young freshman who humiliated the atheist

---

3. As each student stood to acknowledge Josh's supremacy in the battle, I half expected them to proclaim, "O captain, my captain!" in recognition of a key scene in the film *Dead Poet's Society*.

philosophy professor. (Apparently word of Josh's stunning victory has gotten around.)

At the same time that the audience is dutifully texting out the message, Professor Radisson is hit by a car while crossing the street. Two Christians immediately appear on the scene and inform Radisson that he is about to die. Not surprisingly, Professor Radisson does die (presumably because the plot requires it), but not before he has a deathbed conversion to Christianity. Just after he enters eternity, his phone buzzes with a text from one of his concert-going contacts: "God's not dead."

Right! God's not dead. But the one-time atheist professor now is. Get it?! Oh the irony. The entire scenario is a clear riff off the familiar pun:

> "God is dead"—Nietzsche
> "Nietzsche is dead"—God

Just replace "Nietzsche" with "Radisson." Nudge nudge, wink wink.

To sum up, with the character of Professor Radisson *God's Not Dead* portrays atheism as borne of angry rebellion at God and in direct opposition to the overwhelming evidence for God's existence. What is more, Radisson illustrates how atheists aim to suppress the views of others and how they are apt to abandon their skepticism toward God when faced with their own mortality, thereby revealing their atheism as intellectually dishonest.

Like I said, the picture isn't pretty.

Would you marry (vote for or steal the shoes of) an atheist?

The kind of hostility toward atheism that one finds in *God's Not Dead* is an open secret among many atheists. Walter Sinnott-Armstrong captures the antagonism in his book *Morality without God?* with the eye-catching title of the first chapter: "Would You Marry an Atheist?" According to Sinnott-Armstrong, most people would never consider matrimony with an atheist for fear that the atheist spouse "would infect children with depravity and could not be counted on to help with the dishes."[4] The dish washing bit may be tongue-in-cheek, but Sinnott-Armstrong is quite serious about the general societal hostility toward and mistrust of atheists. In support, he points to a 2007 *USA Today*/Gallup poll which asked people whether they would consider voting in an election for candidates under the following list of descriptors: Catholic, female, Mormon, elderly, homosexual, and atheistic.

4. Sinnott-Armstrong, *Morality without God?* 1.

Guess who came in at the very bottom? Yup, a mere 45 percent responded that they would even *consider* voting for an atheist.[5]

Surveys are one way to identify hostile attitudes toward atheists. Another way is by seeing how many atheist labelled shoes disappear in the mail. (Bet you didn't see that one coming!) This story begins with "The Atheist Shoe Company," a unique German start-up business which has distinguished itself in the marketplace by selling comfortable loafers that declare proudly on the tread, "Ich bin Atheist" (German for "I am atheist"). The idea, presumably, is to appeal to the growing market of avowed secular and atheistic people in German society with trendy, secular footwear.[6] Since a growing number of Germans have the designator "atheist" written on their hearts, this company thought it would make sense to put it on their *soles* as well. (My apologies, but I never miss a good chance to use a bad pun.)

Atheism may be on the rise in Europe, but it isn't yet as trendy on the other side of the Atlantic, a fact that The Atheist Shoe Company found out the hard way. While the company regularly ships its unique loafers to secular-minded customers around the world, it began to notice that an inordinately high number of shoes shipped to the United States were not reaching their destination. In their search for an explanation, the company began to suspect the problem lay with the highly visible "atheist" labelled packing tape (a reasonable hypothesis when you're in the land where pastors denounce atheists as "brain dead"). Could it be that the deliveries were being intercepted by pious postal workers who took offense at the prominent display of the word "atheist" on the package?

The resourceful folks at The Atheist Shoe Company put this hypothesis to the test with a clever experiment. They mailed out 178 packages to eighty-nine addresses across the United States with half of the packages wrapped in the distinctive "atheist" tape and the other half wrapped in plain tape. The results were startling: *nine* of the atheist-identified packages never arrived at their destination while only one of the non-atheist packages failed to arrive. In other words, packages marked with the word "atheist" were *nine times* as likely to disappear en route to the shipping address.

5. Ibid., 5.

6. In the last several decades Germany has become increasingly secular. According to a 2005 poll, 25 percent of Germans have no belief in God whatsoever, while an additional 25 percent believe only in some sort of vague life force. See European Commission, "Special Eurobarometer," 9.

In addition, the atheist packages that did arrive took an average of three extra days.[7] The results were too striking to be explained away by chance.

When I blogged on the topic one of my readers, himself an employee of the US Postal Service, was positively indignant. "The mail is sacrosanct," he exclaimed.[8] So what is it about a package labelled "atheist" that could lead an otherwise principled postal worker to violate that sacrosanct duty to deliver the mail? A plausible answer is not hard to find. If atheists are, as many Christians believe, fools who arrogantly suppress the knowledge they have of God, if they really are *brain dead*, and if atheism is nothing more than a cheap cloak for sinful moral rebellion, then it isn't that surprising that some people might see fit to take punitive action against atheists . . . even if that means stealing their shoes!

In sum, Pastor John Hagee's invective against atheists is not all that exceptional. As the movie *God's Not Dead* and the missing atheist shoes suggest, antipathy toward atheism is widespread. Atheists today are viewed with a deep suspicion by the wider population. As atheistic philosopher Louise M. Antony puts it, "We are presumed to be arrogant, devoid of moral sentiments, and insensitive to a wide variety of human goods."[9]

Introducing the Rebellion Thesis . . . and the road ahead

Now that we have a better sense of just how widespread the hostility is toward atheists, we need to ask where it comes from. While there are likely several factors involved, in this book I will be looking at what I believe to be the primary source of this hostility, at least insofar as Christians are concerned. I believe it is ultimately sourced in a set of beliefs about the origin and nature of atheism, a view that I call the Rebellion Thesis. I define the thesis as follows:

> Rebellion Thesis: *While atheists profess to believe that God does not exist, this disbelief is the result of an active and culpable suppression of an innate disposition to believe in God which is borne of a hatred of God and a desire to sin with impunity.*

7. See "Atheist Shoe Co.: Postal Service Discriminating against Shipments to Godless Americans (and the Interesting Way They Say They Found Out)."

8. Rauser, "Does the US Postal Service Discriminate against Atheists?"

9. Antony, "Introduction," in *Philosophers without Gods*, ix.

If the Rebellion Thesis is really this influential in fomenting anger toward and mistrust of atheists then it is important that we understand it. With that in mind, let's take a closer look at this claim. At the core of the Rebellion Thesis is the view that atheists really do possess knowledge of God; At some level they really do *know* he is there, despite all their protestations to the contrary. Consequently, their insistence that God doesn't exist is nothing more than a stubborn refusal to recognize the knowledge of God that they already possess. Though they refuse to admit they have this knowledge, they remain culpable for it.

If you want a poster child for the Rebellion Thesis, think of Professor Radisson the now deceased villain of *God's Not Dead* who was angry at God for the death of his mother and who brashly pronounced himself "God" over his hapless students.

In order to get a fuller grasp on how the Rebellion Thesis depicts the atheist's epistemic situation, let's consider an analogy. Imagine that an office worker so dislikes his boss that every time he hears the man speak over the intercom, he plugs his ears and hums until the boss stops speaking. He can hear the man perfectly well, but he makes every effort to prevent himself from doing so. He may think this excuses him from having to follow the boss's instructions (ignorance is bliss, right?), but he is self-deceived. The boss will still hold him responsible for all the announcements he tried to block out.

This sorry picture gives us a sense of what the Rebellion Thesis proposes. Just as the office worker seeks to block out the voice of the boss he hates, so atheists seek to block out the voice of the God they hate. And just as the office worker is culpable for information he fails to hear because of his stubborn refusal to listen to his boss, so the atheist is culpable for any information she fails to hear because of her stubborn refusal to heed the knowledge of God that she already possesses.

The Rebellion Thesis is a striking claim. And as we have already seen it is a claim that has some currency in contemporary society. But *how many* Christians have taken that view? We will address that question in chapter 2, "April 1st is Atheist Day: Christian attitudes toward atheists," where I will undertake a brief survey of Christian attitudes toward atheism from the eighteenth century down to today. In the chapter I will demonstrate that the Rebellion Thesis has been widely accepted by Christian theologians and church leaders, and I will do so by surveying some influential Christian leaders over the last three centuries who have expressed views supportive of the Rebellion Thesis. Once we have established that leading pastors and theologians have endorsed the Rebellion Thesis, it is not a stretch to assume that many average people (including those who go to Christian movies and those who sort your mail) have dutifully followed suit.

If Christians have widely held the Rebellion Thesis, the next question to consider is whether they have had good reason to do so. And that leads us to ask: how would a Christian propose to establish the truth of the Rebellion Thesis? We will begin to tackle this question in chapter 3, "Does the Bible say atheists are fools?," by evaluating the biblical evidence for the Rebellion Thesis. In this chapter we will assay the main biblical passages that are invoked in support of the thesis, including Psalm 14:1, Ephesians 2:12, and Romans 1:18–21. My argument will be that, contrary to popular opinion, these texts do not address the intellectual atheism of modern Western society—e.g., the belief that no God exists—and so *they offer no direct support for the Rebellion Thesis.* While the most promising text for the Rebellion Thesis is Romans 1:18–21, I will argue that any attempt to appeal to this text to justify the thesis has the devastating consequence of turning all doubt and questioning—including the doubts that are a reality for millions of Christians—into a matter of sinful rebellion.

Even if the Bible lacks the evidence to support the Rebellion Thesis, a Christian could still possibly mount a modest empirical defense for it based on real world interaction with atheists. For example, if atheists consistently demonstrated a hatred of God and a refusal to believe in him—if every atheist behaved like Professor Radisson—then that evidence could be marshalled in support of the Rebellion Thesis. We will put that approach to the test over two chapters, starting in chapter 4, "Do atheists have an axe to grind?" In this chapter I will undertake a modest exploration both of the rationality of atheism and the psychological disposition of a token atheist by way of an extended conversation with atheist Jeffery Jay Lowder. For some years now, Lowder has been a vocal and vigorous defender of atheism in various capacities, including author, debater, and blogger. In addition, Lowder was the co-founder of Internet Infidels way back in 1995. Not only does Lowder have the intellectual acumen to defend the rationality of an atheistic worldview, but he also does so in a deeply thoughtful, charitable, and irenic manner. The fact that there are atheists like Lowder who provide a formidable defense of atheism without rancor provides evidence against the Rebellion Thesis.

Some atheists do seem to make claims consistent with the Rebellion Thesis, and indeed those claims have often been cited by Christians as evidence for the thesis. In chapter 5, "What about the atheists who say they don't want there to be a God?," we will ask whether particular high profile cases of atheists who express hostility toward God could provide any support for the Rebellion Thesis. I will argue that they don't for at least two reasons. First, even if *some* atheists are in rebellion against God, it doesn't follow that *all* are. Second, in many cases it is very difficult, if not impossible, to discern when hostility is directed against God and when it may have another target, such as Christians who failed to live out their faith.

I began this book with a retelling of the Parable of the Good Samaritan. In the day and age in which Jesus spoke, the very idea of a "good" Samaritan was an oxymoron. For Jesus's first-century Jewish audience, Samaritans were despised and distrusted social pariahs on the periphery of good Jewish society. So for Jesus to place a Samaritan in the "hero" role, and then contrast that with the religious hypocrisy of the Jewish leaders, amounted to a polemical shot across the bow of the religious status quo.

These days within the Christian community, especially within North America, the atheist has assumed the mantle of the despised and distrusted social pariah on the margins. Just as first-century Jews needed to repent of prejudices against Samaritans, so today contemporary Christians need to repent of prejudices against atheists. In our final chapter, "The atheist as neighbor," we shall turn back to the lessons of that parable as we seek to recast the Christian engagement with the atheist in the terms of a rediscovered hospitality. On this point we will follow the lead of Pope Francis who has shown an admirable openness to atheists, which, as we will see, has been reciprocated in surprising ways.

Like two roads diverging in the wood, John Hagee and Pope Francis represent two very different approaches to Christian engagement with the atheist community. One road dismisses atheists as brain dead and tells them to get out of the country. The other road embraces them with kindness as true neighbors. I believe it's time for Christians to repent of their prejudices and take the road less travelled. The atheist *is* our neighbor, and this book explains why.

2

April 1st is Atheist Day
Christian attitudes toward atheists

We live in an age where complex issues are often reduced to bumper stickers. This trend definitely has its downsides. After all, the bumper sticker slogan is hardly a good way to seek nuance. But there is also an upside to bumper stickers since they can provide a terse and memorable introduction to a particular attitude or perspective. And so it is for the Rebellion Thesis. If you want to find a succinct statement of the sentiment, you need look no further than the sticker I first saw pasted on the back of a rusty Ford Tempo:

> **April 1st is Atheist Day: Psalm 14:1**

That certainly qualifies as terse and memorable. Right there you have in one sentence a succinct summary of the common Christian attitude toward atheists. The logic seems to work like this: Psalm 14:1 declares, "The fool has said in his heart, there is no God." Since atheists say in their heart that there is no God, it must follow that atheists are fools. And since April 1st is April *Fools'* Day, it follows that April 1st is the special day for atheists. (At this point the Christians laugh and high five one another.)

This phrase isn't just a punch-line, for it turns out that there is a popular story that goes with it. According to that story, an atheist plaintiff went to court protesting religious discrimination on the grounds that Christians and Jews have their own public holidays, but there is no public holiday for atheists. The judge promptly threw out the case with the quip that atheists *do* have their own holiday . . . April 1st!

Insert laugh track here

The "foolish atheist" story circulates among Christians in several slightly amended forms. For example, in her book *The One Year Devos for Teens*, Susie Shellenberger includes a devotional reflection titled "Don't be a fool!" that begins with a slightly different take on the story. On this version, an atheist sitting on an airplane complains to his neighbor that atheists don't have any holidays like Christians. Shellenberger observes: "The man seated behind them couldn't help overhearing their conversation. He leaned forward and said, 'There's always April Fool's Day.'"[1]

My first response to this story is disgust at the obnoxious way the man in the back row interrupts a private conversation simply to insult one of the speakers. What kind of example is that? But Shellenberger doesn't seem to be particularly worried about how Miss Manners might assess the situation. She concludes the devotional by issuing a sober challenge to her young readers: "You have a choice: You can look stupid in the eyes of the world and be a fool for Jesus. Or you can embrace your culture and its beliefs and be a fool for eternity."[2] I guess that's one way to look at it. But I still think the behavior of the obnoxious fellow in the back is a bad lesson for kids.

In Shellenberger's devotional, the story seems to be presented as a fictionalized anecdote to make a teaching point. In other renditions, the story functions merely as a humorous "Christian" joke at the expense of a minority group. However, I have also seen the foolish atheist story (in one or another of its various iterations) relayed as if it were a real historical event. At that point it morphs from a mere anecdote or punch-line into an urban legend.[3]

Here's a question for us: Why does the foolish atheist story get traded around in the first place? Why would Christians think this story is funny, or wise, or thought-provoking, or poignant, or otherwise worthwhile to share? I would think the answer is quite obvious. In the same way that an inappropriate ethnic joke that quickly makes the rounds can illustrate latent racist attitudes in a community, so it is with inappropriate atheist jokes that

1. Shellenberger, *The One Year Devos for Teens*, 95.

2. Ibid.

3. See "Judges 5:31," snopes.com.

are embraced by Christians. In short, it would appear that the enthusiasm with which Christian communities embrace this anecdote is indicative of some preexistent prejudicial hostility toward atheists.

It is worth noting that the hostility many Christians have toward atheists is not new. In his entry on "atheism" in the influential 1967 *Encyclopedia of Philosophy*, Paul Edwards includes a subsection titled "Hostility to Atheism" where he observes:

> One could fill many volumes with the abuse and calumny contained in the writings of Christian apologists, learned no less than popular. The tenor of these writings is not simply that atheism is mistaken but also that only a depraved person could adopt so hideous a position . . . .[4]

Edwards backs up his assessment by providing a list of several influential Christians from previous centuries who have expressed scathing opinions toward atheism. For example, Richard Bentley (1662–1742) argued that no atheist could be a "true friend" or "loyal subject." Meanwhile, John Locke (1632–1704), the great philosopher and peerless campaigner for religious tolerance, staunchly refused to extend that toleration to atheists. And that's just the beginning. By the end of the section, Edwards has provided us with a substantial and sobering amount of evidence for the pervasive influence of the Rebellion Thesis within modern Christendom.

In order to get a better grasp on the Rebellion Thesis and its influence in modern Christianity we will focus in this chapter on the commentary various Protestant Christians have made about atheists from the seventeenth century down to today. To be sure, Protestants have hardly cornered the market on atheist-hostilities. Julian Baggini, the popular atheistic philosopher, recalls the perception of atheism he gleaned while growing up in the Catholic Church. He writes, "Belief in God and obedience to his will was constitutive of our conception of goodness, and therefore any belief that rejected God was by definition opposed to the good. Atheists could only belong to the dark side."[5] Now looking back upon his Catholic upbringing Baggini concludes that "they succeeded in forging an association between atheism and the sinister, the negative, and the evil."[6] Suffice it to say, antagonism toward atheism is certainly not limited to Protestant Christianity, even if our focus shall be.

4. Edwards, "Atheism," in *The Encyclopedia of Philosophy*, 174.

5. Baggini, *Atheism:*, 1–2.

6. Ibid., 2.

The Rebellion Thesis in Protestant history

We begin our journey with the great Puritan theologian and philosopher Stephen Charnock (1628–80), whose monumental treatise *The Existence and Attributes of God* can still be read with profit today (especially if you can get somebody to pay you to read it!). Charnock wrote at a time when atheism and skepticism were just emerging as live intellectual options among the cultured elites of Europe. However, he clearly had little sympathy with atheism as an intellectual position. Charnock points out that theism has been universally held, "by the wise and ignorant, by the learned and stupid, by those who had no other guide but the dimmest light of nature . . . ."[7] The reason for this agreement is simple: No rational person can deny that God exists. As Charnock put it, "Men that will not listen to Scripture, as having no counterpart of it in their souls, cannot easily deny natural reason, which riseth up on all sides for the justification of this truth."[8]

While atheism wouldn't become a significant intellectual movement within Europe until decades after Charnock's death, there were a few atheists in his day. You might think, then, that this fact would present a challenge to his assertion that theism is universal. However, Charnock is ready for this rejoinder with the retort that the exception does not disprove the rule: "Why should . . . the exceptions of a few, not one to millions, discredit that which is voted certainly true by the joint consent of the world?"[9] Think about it like this: If 999,999 people insist they heard a loud explosion and only one detractor claims he heard nothing, it is most reasonable to conclude that the 999,999 are correct. As for the one detractor, he's likely either cognitively impaired (e.g., deaf) or a liar. And so it goes for atheism. For Charnock, the one thing we can be sure of is that atheism is absolutely irrational and indefensible on any intellectual ground. He writes:

> For the first, every atheist is a grand fool. If he were not a fool, he would not imagine a thing so contrary to the stream of the universal reason of the world, contrary to the rational dictates of his own soul, and contrary to the testimony of every creature, and link in the chain of creation: if he were not a fool, he would not strip himself of humanity, and degrade himself lower than the most despicable brute.[10]

7. Charnock, *The Existence and Attributes of God*, I, 30.
8. Ibid., 37.
9. Ibid., 33.
10. Ibid., 25.

These are strong words. According to Charnock, not only is atheism foolish and unreasonable, it also constitutes a flat denial of one's very humanity, an intellectual position so debased that one can adopt it only by lowering oneself below even "the most despicable brute."

Our second example comes from a contemporary of Charnock, the scientist Robert Boyle (1627–91). While Boyle is most famous for his work in chemistry, he also wrote in theology and spent years working on a treatise against atheism. While he never completed the work, Boyle's notes provide a helpful snapshot of the great scientist's view of atheism. In the section titled "The Character of the Atheist," he describes the atheist as a wicked person seeking to be free of the chains of conscience (please note that I have left the archaic seventeenth-century spelling and punctuation of the quotation unmodified):

> For not only 'tis the Interest as well as 'tis the desire of wicked men as wicked that there should be no God to awe them, no Conscience to curb or molest them, nor no Law to condemne them. But men even as men are naturally prone to affect Independency & Liberty in their Actions, & are unwilling to be ty'd to give an account of themselves or what they doe to any but themselves.[11]

Boyle believed that atheists have no interest in pursuing or knowing the truth, and that their atheism was a result of their active will to suppress their conscience borne of the desire not to be accountable to anybody for the lives they live. In short, he views the atheist in the mold of Herod Antipas who cynically retorted "What is truth?" In the same manner the atheist shows no genuine interest in really knowing the way things are:

> Too many bad men seek Truth as Insyncerely, as Herod did him that justly call'd himself Truth. For as that Tyrant seem'd very solicitous to find out Christ that he might submit himself to him, and worship him; but indeed intended to destroy him: So the bad men I speak of, make a great shew of diligently searching for Truth and highly respecting it, but in reality intend but to destroy it, or oppose it.[12]

Boyle's bleak assessment of atheism is perhaps best summarized in the following memorable analogy: "Atheism and vice (especially Sensuality and

---

11. Boyle, *Boyle on Atheism*, 163.
12. Ibid., 165.

Pride) beget one another (like water and Ice)."[13] Sounds to me like we might have another Rebellion Thesis bumper sticker here: "Atheism and vice are like water and ice."

Before we move on to our next example, we will pause for a moment to take note of the entry on "atheism" in the 1771 edition of *Encyclopedia Britannica*. The entry reads, "Many people, both ancient and modern, have pretended to atheism, or have been reckoned atheists by the world; but it is justly questioned whether any man seriously adopted such a principle. These pretensions, therefore, must be founded on pride or affection."[14] Note how closely this passage aligns with the Rebellion Thesis. Atheism is a disingenuous position carried by sinful pride. And given that this comes from a source as prestigious as the *Encyclopedia Britannica*, one can surmise that such assumptions were in wide circulation in the late eighteenth century.

For our third example we will move ahead one century and over to North America to consider Timothy Dwight IV (1752–1817), a renowned American Congregationalist theologian and pastor who served as president of Yale College from 1795 until his death in 1817. Dwight was an especially accomplished sermonizer, as one can see in his popular work *Theology: Explained and Defended, in a Series of Sermons*. His treatment of atheism within this work is harsh and to the point. Dwight shares Charnock and Boyle's assessment of the atheist as immoral. Consequently, he concludes that atheists "have ever been corrupt; they have ever done abominable works; there has never been among them a single good or virtuous man."[15] Like Charnock and Boyle, Dwight impugns the moral state of any individual who would identify as an atheist as being in sinful rebellion.

Our next stop on the journey brings us several decades further on and back over to England as we consider arguably the most striking and disturbing portrait of the atheist in our survey. That picture comes from our next interlocutor, the great Baptist pastor of nineteenth-century England, Charles Spurgeon (1834–92). Often called "the Prince of Preachers," Spurgeon proclaimed the word weekly to thousands at New Park Street Chapel, and he did so for nearly forty years. It is estimated that by the time of his death he had preached to close to *ten million* people,[16] to say nothing

---

13. Ibid., 166.

14. Cited in Berman, *A History of Atheism in Britain*, 1.

15. Dwight, *Theology: Explained and Defended*, 100.

16. Harmon, *Spurgeon*, 13.

of the tens of millions who have been (and continue to be) impacted by his voluminous writing.

Among Spurgeon's many popular works was the three-volume *Treasury of David*, an expansive commentary on the Psalms, which remains a strong seller to this day. When we turn to his discussion of Psalm 14:1 within the *Treasury*, we find him going even further than Charnock, Boyle, and Dwight in impugning the character of the atheist. Not only does he assert that the atheist is lower than the "most despicable brute," Spurgeon goes even further, insisting that the atheist is even *lower than the demons of hell*. Lower than demons? That *is* low! How does Spurgeon defend such a woefully bleak appraisal of atheism? He explains:

> The devils believe and acknowledge four articles of our faith (Matt. 8:29): (1) They acknowledge God; (2) Christ; (3) the day of judgment; (4) that they shall be tormented then; so that he that does not believe there is a God is more vile than a devil. To deny there is a God is a sort of atheism that is not to be found in hell.[17]

While Spurgeon does not render his reasoning explicit, it would appear that he relies on a principle like this:

> Spurgeon's Principle: *If a human person fails to accept a true doctrinal belief that a demon accepts then the human person is viler than the demon.*

Thus, because the atheist lacks a true doctrinal belief that the demon accepts—namely "God exists"—it follows that the human person is worse (that is, viler) than the demon.

It doesn't take much reflection to see that Spurgeon's Principle quickly leads to absurdities. We can begin with the fact that Christianity is full of opposing theological camps: Calvinists vs. Arminians, pedobaptists vs. believer's baptists, charismatics vs. cessationists, and so on. In each case, the devils presumably know which side is correct in the theological dispute and which side is in error. And since it is highly likely that all Christians are wrong about at least some of their doctrinal views, it follows that every Christian lacks at least some true beliefs that the devils possess. From this it follows, based on Spurgeon's Principle, that *all Christians are viler than the devils*.

That's what we call being *hoist with one's own petard*. In other words, you aim to toss an incendiary device to smoke somebody else and it ends

---

17. Spurgeon, *The Treasury of David*, 59.

up exploding in your face. It's also called sawing off the branch you're sitting on. And cutting off your nose to spite your face. And a few other things. In short, it isn't good.

Consequently, Spurgeon's Principle is bad news for the Christians. But it gets worse yet. You see, the devils would also have true beliefs about God (e.g., the Trinity; incarnation) which were not held by any of the Old Testament saints—Abraham, Moses, David, etc. And so, the Christian who endorses Spurgeon's Principle would be obliged to conclude that *the Old Testament saints were also viler than devils*. But surely this is absurd.

At this point it would appear that the best course for the Christian is to reject Spurgeon's Principle. In other words, we should recognize that the failure to accept every true belief about God that a demon holds does *not* make you viler than the demon. However, rejecting Spurgeon's Principle in order to defend Christian ignorance about various theological claims requires us to accept that non-Christians (including atheists) likewise cannot be censured for ignorance. Given that there is nothing to commend Spurgeon's spurious reasoning, it would appear to amount to little more than a lowbrow attempt quite literally to *demonize* atheists.

Not content to leave things there, Spurgeon then seeks to drive home his point regarding the immorality of atheists by providing an extended quotation from the famous eighteenth-century English essayist, Joseph Addison (1672–1719). It is worth noting that Addison penned the lyrics for the famous hymn "The Spacious Firmament on High," which poetically describes the way that creation testifies to God's existence and goodness:

> The spacious firmament on high,
> With all the blue ethereal sky,
> And spangled heav'ns, a shining flame,
> Their great Original proclaim.
> The unwearied sun from day to day
> Does his Creator's power display,
> And publishes to every land
> The works of an almighty hand.

It is worth taking note of this fact because Addison's hymn contains one of the most eloquent descriptions of God's general revelation in the English language. Day and night the firmament above proclaims its Creator, vividly displaying his power to people from every land. This is some highfalutin hymnody!

So what happens when Addison encounters a person who doesn't share his perspective on the overwhelming general revelation of creation? What happens when he finds somebody who doesn't agree that the skies proclaim "Their great Original"? We get our answer in Spurgeon's quote where Addison shares his recollections of one particular, cowardly atheist that he encountered on a sailing ship many years earlier. Addison writes:

> In distresses, the atheist must be of all creatures the most helpless and forlorn. About thirty years ago, I was a shipboard with one of these vermin, when there arose a brisk gale, which could frighten nobody but himself. Upon the rolling of the ship he fell upon his knees and confessed to the chaplain that he had been a vile atheist and had denied a supreme Being ever since he came to his estate.
>
> The good man was astonished, and a report immediately ran through the ship that there was an atheist upon the upper deck. Several of the common seamen, who had never heard the word before, thought it had been some strange fish; but they were more surprised when they saw it was a man and heard out of his own mouth "that he never believed till that day that there was a God."
>
> As he lay in the agonies of confession, one of the honest tars whispered to the boatswain "that it would be a good deed to heave him overboard." But we were now within sight of port, when of a sudden the wind fell, and the penitent relapsed, begging of all of us that were present as we were gentlemen not to say anything of what had passed.
>
> He had not been ashore above two days when one of the company began to rally him upon his devotion on shipboard, which the other denied in so high terms that it produced the lie on both sides and ended in a duel. The atheist was run through the body, and after some loss of blood, became as good a Christian as he was at sea till he found that his wound was not mortal.[18]

So that's the picture. And it's definitely ugly. Remember, this passage is offered as a sort of explanatory expansion of Spurgeon's claim that atheists are worse than devils. Given that this is such a revealing quote we should spend some time reflecting on it. And we can begin with Addison's striking decision to refer to the atheist with the dehumanizing descriptors "creature" and "vermin." As we proceed, we'll focus in on the incendiary term "vermin." This term has two basic meanings:

---

18. Cited in Spurgeon, *The Treasury of David*, 60.

> vermin: 1 wild mammals and birds which are harmful to crops, farm animals, or game or which carry disease; parasitic worms or insects. 2 very unpleasant or destructive people.[19]

The second definition functioned originally as an analogical extension of the first definition and the practice of referring to human beings as vermin has a horrifying history in the modern age. In the twentieth century génocidaires have often referred to the out-groups they sought to annihilate as vermin, most infamously in the case of Nazi anti-Semitic propaganda. As Caroline Alice Wiedmer observes:

> Vermin such as spiders and rats were the common figures for Jews in Nazi propaganda, and the German populace was supposed to define the Jews as inhuman and parasitic, as vermin to be feared and ultimately destroyed—robbed of all personal belongings and put into gas chambers to be exterminated with pesticide. The distinction between tenor and vehicle was no longer upheld during the Third Reich because the vermin metaphor was made literal in the Nazis' treatment of the Jews.[20]

This practice of dehumanizing out-groups by labelling them as creatures, vermin, or some other form of pestilence has been a common feature of genocides throughout history. Gregory H. Stanton, founder and president of Genocide Watch, observes that in the lead up to genocide it is common that members of a target group "are equated with animals, vermin, insects or diseases. Dehumanization overcomes the normal human revulsion against murder."[21]

In case you're wondering whether the meaning of the term vermin might have shifted since Addison's day, the answer is no. According to the *Online Etymology Dictionary*, the term's application to describe noxious animals dates to the 1300s while its analogical extension to human beings dates at least to the 1560s.[22] So the rhetorical punch that the term carries

---

19. "Vermin," in *Concise Oxford English Dictionary*, 1607.

20. Wiedmer, *The Claims of Memory*, 3.

21. Cited in Smith, *Why We Demean, Enslave, and Exterminate Others*, 142. Social scientists Clark McCauley and Daniel Chirot add, "In most genocidal events the perpetrators devalue the humanity of their victims, often by referring to the victims as animals, diseased, or exceptionally filthy . . . notably pigs, rats, maggots, cockroaches, and other vermin." Cited in Smith, *Why We Demean, Enslave, and Exterminate Others*, 142.

22. "Vermin," in *Online Etymology Dictionary*. Samuel Johnson's famous dictionary, published less than forty years after Addison's death, defines "vermin" as "any noxious animal." See *Johnson's Dictionary*, 380.

today approximated that of Addison's own day. In short, referring to atheists as vermin was every bit as shocking and dehumanizing in Addison's age as it is in ours.

It seems to me that this kind of labelling of entire groups of people (whether the group is defined in terms of ethnicity, gender, socio-economic class, religion . . . or *irreligion*) as "creatures" or "vermin" is cause for the highest concern. Sadly, reading through Addison's entire account makes it clear that the use of this terminology was not a mere anomaly. Instead, it frames the entire discussion as part of an extended effort to objectify and dehumanize atheists. As he continues he goes on to describe this atheist on the ship as cowardly and unscrupulous. As a visual illustration of his point, Addison observes that the moment a wind began to blow on the ship the atheist was the first—and only—person who was fearful. In fact, this modest breeze was sufficient for the atheist to renounce his atheism posthaste, thereby revealing his unbelief to be a superficial charade. Addison then reiterates the same point at the end of the passage by noting that the atheist once again renounced his beliefs when he was wounded in a duel. Perhaps this all happened just as described, but one could be forgiven for suspecting that Addison has embellished the events somewhat so as to paint the atheist in the worst possible light.

The description of the atheist's insufferable cowardice coupled with his alleged willingness to turn to God when under duress conveys a picture of atheism as tantamount to childish rebellion; as we say in modern parlance, "there are no atheists in foxholes." Since I brought up that old adage, it is worth pointing out that in fact there *are* some atheists in foxholes (though I can't claim to know how many). To note but one significant and high profile example: the documentary *Touching the Void* tells the story of the ill-fated mountain climbing expedition of Joe Simpson and Simon Yates in the Peruvian Andes. At one point high on the mountain Simpson falls to the bottom of a deep crevasse. In the film he reflects that as he lay there in the darkness, thinking he would soon face death, he never once considered returning to belief in God: "I was brought up as a devout Catholic. I'd long since stopped believing in God. I always wondered if things really hit the fan, whether I would, under pressure, turn around and say, you know, a few Hail Marys and say 'Get me out of here.' It never once occurred to me."[23] The stoic atheistic mountaineer of *Touching the Void* who faces his fate with equanimity certainly paints a different picture of an atheist than Addison's

23. *Touching the Void*. Directed by Kevin Macdonald. 2003

cowardly seaman who forsakes his skepticism the moment a moderate breeze nudges the hull of the ship.[24]

By the way, do you think that Addison and Spurgeon would have been fazed by the *Touching the Void* example? I suspect not. Instead, I bet they'd simply attribute Simpson's unwavering atheism in the face of death to the depth of his depravity and rebellion. And that leaves us with a classic damned-if-you-do, damned-if-you-don't scenario: if the atheist surrenders his belief while under threat, as did the atheist in Addison's anecdote, then he's a disingenuous coward. But if he retains it, as did Simpson, then he is depraved and rebellious. Either way, the poor atheist can't win!

Perhaps the most disturbing aspect of Addison's narrative (and Spurgeon's appropriation of it) is the tacit commendation of violence against atheists. When Addison recalls that one of the sailors crudely suggests that the atheist be tossed overboard like any other vermin, Addison doesn't rebuke him. Instead, he laments the fact that this "honest" sailor made the suggestion when they were "already in sight of the port," thereby suggesting that this was a lost opportunity. As shocking as that sentiment is, when Spurgeon quotes this passage he doesn't distance himself from this reprehensible, hate-filled characterization of atheists and the equally reprehensible tacit approval of violence against them. Instead, he quotes this entire passage with approval. Finally, keep in mind that he quotes it within the confines of an *inspirational devotional biblical commentary*, and all to support his spurious claim that atheists are worse than demons, itself an absurd charge.

Obviously these five voices—Charnock, Boyle, Addison, Dwight, and Spurgeon—do not speak for all Christians in their respective time periods. Nonetheless, each was an influential and highly esteemed Christian leader of his day: a philosopher, a scientist, an essayist, a theologian, and a pastor. What is perhaps most telling is that each states his views on atheism matter-of-factly with no sense of straying far from popular opinion or courting controversy. In conclusion, this brief survey provides solid evidence that prior to the twentieth century the Rebellion Thesis was widely embraced by (Protestant) Christians.

---

24. For further discussion, see myths 18 and 19 in Blackford and Schüklenk, *50 Great Myths about Atheism*.

The Rebellion Thesis Today

Now that we are at the end of our brief historical survey we can turn to our own day by considering contemporary attitudes toward atheism. Here the question is whether the opinions of John Hagee and *God's Not Dead* represent an anomaly left over from an earlier age, or whether they represent attitudes that persist widely into our own day.

So far as I can see, the negative views of atheism appear to have diversified and softened somewhat in our age. (For example, it's thankfully much harder to find Christians who denounce atheists as vermin or who lament the lost opportunity to toss an atheist overboard!) However, look closer and one finds that the Rebellion Thesis continues to be widely endorsed by key Christian leaders. As evidence of this fact, in this section we will survey some contemporary conservative evangelicals to see their view of atheism.

We will begin our contemporary survey with the popular evangelist and apologist Grant Jeffrey. During his lifetime (Jeffrey passed away suddenly in 2012) Jeffrey sold several million books on a range of topics, including end times prophecy and apologetics. In his book *The Signature of God,* Jeffrey explains why he had given up even trying to reason with atheists:

> Now when I get into a discussion with an atheist or an agnostic, I simply respond as follows: "I will not debate you about whether God exists for the same reason that I would not debate someone about whether the world is round. I believe that those who claim, 'There is no God,' in the face of overwhelming evidence found throughout nature are either fools or liars. Any person who honestly believes that all of the marvelous complexity of this universe simply happened by chance is a fool. If he is not a fool, yet still claims to believe that this incredibly complex universe is a result of random chance, then I must conclude that he is not being honest. In either case it is clearly a waste of time to argue the obvious."[25]

Note the stark alternative that Jeffrey presents: Atheists are either fools (and so cognitively deficient) or liars (and thereby morally deficient). Jeffrey believes these are the only choices because, as he sees it, no rational and morally upright person could possibly deny God's existence given the objective evidence available in the world.

25. Jeffrey, *The Signature of God,* 20–21.

Ray Comfort, another apologist well known for his brusque, direct style, states his view of atheism in the title of his book *You Can Lead an Atheist to Evidence But You Can't Make Him Think*. With a title like that, it should be no surprise that Comfort echoes Jeffrey's opinion that no reasonable and moral person could possibly deny the existence of God. As he puts it, "Creation is *absolute* proof that there is a Creator. You cannot have a creation without a Creator. It is impossible ('Then who made God?' has a logical answer). End of argument; unless, according to the Bible, you are a fool (read Psalm 14:1 and Romans 1:20)."[26] For Comfort there is no room for debate and no need for qualification. One's choice is stark: accept the obvious truth of theism or deny it and show yourself to be a fool. In keeping with this brusque style, Comfort concludes his book *God Doesn't Believe in Atheists* with a challenge to his atheist readers (assuming Comfort *has* any atheist readers): "At least be true to yourself and drop your 'atheist' label. You are just using the word as a very weak and transparent shield for sin."[27]

Next up, we have D. James Kennedy. Kennedy was a popular author, broadcaster of the television program *The Coral Ridge Hour*, and pastor of Coral Ridge Presbyterian Church in Florida. In short, he was widely recognized as one of the most influential evangelical leaders in North America. To get a sense of his reputation, the day after Kennedy died in 2007 the White House issued a press release expressing the sadness of President and Mrs. Bush at his passing. Kennedy wrote often about apologetics. When he turns to discussing atheism in chapter 3 of his book *The Presence of a Hidden God*, there is no mistaking his personal assessment. The chapter, provocatively titled "Atheism: Religion of Fools," begins with a limerick:

> There once was an atheist who did crow
> "There's no place above or below."
> And so when he died,
> The minister sighed,
> "All dressed up, and no place to go!"[28]

No doubt many of Kennedy's readers found this poem to be nothing more than an amusing anecdote at the expense of the godless. You can bet that few if any would have ever stopped to consider that it might be offensive. But let's turn the tables for the moment. Imagine if an atheist titled

---

26. Comfort, *You Can Lead an Atheist to Evidence But you Can't Make Him Think*, 3.

27. Comfort, *God Doesn't Believe in Atheists*, 178.

28. Kennedy, *The Presence of a Hidden God*, 35.

a book chapter "Christianity: Religion of Fools" and then prefaced it with *this* limerick:

> There once was a Christian who did crow
> "When I die I know where *I'll* go."
> Then he died without a sound,
> and turned to worm food in the ground.
> All dressed up, and no place to go!

I have no doubt that most Christians would not find this chapter title or limerick to be amusing, let alone helpful in facilitating a thoughtful and charitable engagement with Christian views. Indeed, they'd probably find it tactless, if not downright offensive! And they'd be right. With that in mind, we need only apply the Golden Rule to Kennedy's original limerick: if you don't like being mocked or belittled then don't mock or belittle others. It's that simple.

Not surprisingly, Kennedy's opening limerick sets the tone for the irreverent and uncharitable portrait of atheism that he paints in the chapter. Indeed, "uncharitable" is just the starting point: Kennedy occasionally lurches beyond the discourteous to the point of baldly perpetuating outright falsehoods. For example, he asserts, "If there's anything the atheist can't stand, it's the idea that we have some purpose in our lives."[29] This is a jaw-dropping statement. Note the absoluteness of Kennedy's claim: he wants us to believe that atheists *en masse* are strongly opposed to the very idea of purposeful lives. Not only is this statement false, but it is truly astounding in its disconnection with the diverse and thoughtful opinions of real atheists. In fact, atheist literature is replete with serious attempts to account for a sense of genuine meaning, value, and purpose in a godless universe. For example, Richard Dawkins, the most famous atheist in the world today, devoted an entire book, *The Magic of Reality: How We Know What's Real*, to explain what he understands meaning and purpose to be. He writes:

> We are moved to tears by a beautiful piece of music and we describe the performance as "magical." We gaze up at the stars on a dark night with no moon and no city lights and, breathless with joy, we say the sight is "pure magic." We might use the same word to describe a gorgeous sunset, or an alpine landscape, or a rainbow against a dark sky. In this sense, "magical" simply means deeply moving, exhilarating: something that gives us goose bumps,

29. Kennedy, *The Presence of a Hidden God,* 40.

something that makes us feel more fully alive. What I hope to show you in this book is that reality—the facts of the real world as understood through the methods of science—is magical in this . . . poetic sense, the good to be alive sense.[30]

Atheists like Dawkins don't reject meaning and purpose. Indeed, one of the reasons they are hostile to organized religion is precisely *because they believe it provides a false and harmful understanding of meaning and purpose.* To be sure, a Christian can certainly take issue with that assessment of Christianity (or religion). They can also take issue with the adequacy of various atheistic theories of meaning. But no *informed* Christian can honestly deny that very many atheists remain deeply committed to the pursuit of meaning and purpose.

As the chapter progresses, Kennedy continues to caricature and misrepresent the positions of atheists. For example, he asserts that atheists deny free will and reduce the mind to "brain-bile we ooze out, which causes us to do things we have no control over."[31] Ugh. This is another grossly uncharitable caricature and it is worthwhile to take a moment to unpack (and deconstruct) it. Kennedy's comment touches on two issues, theories of free will and theories of mind.

Let's start with the issue of free will. On this topic, philosophers wrestle with two basic questions:

1. Are we determined to make the choices we make?

2. Are we free to make the choices we make?

The first thing to note here is that Christians disagree on how to answer both of these questions. Some Christians believe that human beings are determined by prior causes (in particular the divine cause, God) while others deny this. Further, some Christians affirm that human beings are free while others deny this.[32] But Christians aren't the only ones to disagree on these matters, for atheists do as well. Some atheists affirm determinism while others deny it. Some atheists affirm free will while others deny it.

---

30. Dawkins, *The Magic of Reality*, 21. While *The Magic of Reality* was published after Kennedy's book, Dawkins covers some similar ground in his earlier book *Unweaving the Rainbow*. See also Dworkin, *Religion without God*; Comte-Sponville, *The Little Book of Atheist Spirituality*; Harris, *Waking Up*.

31. Kennedy, *The Presence of a Hidden God*, 41.

32. Martin Luther famously rejected free will over-against his rival Erasmus in his 1525 book *The Bondage of the Will*. Among contemporary Christian philosophers who explicitly reject free will, one could consider Derk Pereboom, *Living Without Free Will*.

The simple lesson is that one cannot draw any divide between atheists and Christians based on their respective attitudes to either determinism or free will.

Now let's turn to the second issue on which Kennedy's quote touches, that is, the nature of the mind. As we saw, Kennedy baldly claims that atheists believe the mind is nothing more than "brain-bile" oozing out of our cranium. Let me start by saying that I have never read any philosopher of mind, atheist or otherwise, who describes the mind in these terms. The philosophy of mind is focused on basic questions like the following:

1. Is the mind a substance distinct from the body?

2. Are conscious events reducible to physical events?

As with free will, so it is with consciousness, we find a diversity of opinion among theistic and atheistic philosophers of mind on both questions. These days most atheistic philosophers of mind would answer (1) negatively, but many theistic (and Christian) philosophers of mind would agree with them. Regarding (2), opinions are more evenly split. Some atheistic philosophers of mind would defend the reducibility of mental events, but others would not. And the same is true of theistic (and Christian) philosophers of mind. Consequently, Kennedy's characterization of atheistic views of the mind is pure invention.

Next, Kennedy alleges that atheism will have negative social consequences, and he presents as evidence a decline in the willingness of people to take responsibility for their own actions. As he puts it, "This has gone so far that today we have 'the victim defense' which is, 'The victim made me do it. It's all the fault of that corpse I killed.'"[33] Let's assume, for the sake of argument, that Kennedy is correct that there has been a statistically significant decline in personal responsibility in modern society. Even so, he has hardly demonstrated that this decline is directly caused by the spread of *atheism*. He simply assumes it. That's bad enough, but to make matters worse, Kennedy has also committed what philosophers call the fallacy of the single cause by assuming without evidence that the complex phenomenon of declining personal responsibility in society is all attributable to a single (i.e., atheistic) cause.

I am taking the time to critique the details of Kennedy's characterization of atheism for the purposes of illustration. Sadly, the fact is that such flippant caricaturing of atheism remains distressingly common among

---

33. Ibid., 41.

Christian leaders. Not surprisingly, many atheists have responded in kind with the new atheists in particular invoking an endless cascade of caricatures of Christianity and religious faith.[34] But it should hardly need to be pointed out that this doesn't mean Christians are permitted to act in the same manner. Christians are supposed to have rejected "tit-for-tat" justice in favor of seventy-times-seven forgiveness. As everybody's mom taught them, two wrongs don't make a right. And as Jesus instructed us, we ought to do to others as we would like others to do to us. So if Christians are offended when atheists caricature their views, then Christians should be vigilant about not replying in kind.

Our next example comes from Dan DeHaan (d. 1982), the founder of the organization Training Church Leaders. His final book, *The God You Can Know*, features a glowing forward by J. I. Packer, one of the most influential Protestant evangelical theologians and church leaders of the last fifty years. In the book DeHaan notes that there are some people who are honest agnostics.[35] In other words, DeHaan seems to recognize that people can have genuine doubts about whether God exists. But, he insists, the situation is quite different for atheism: in DeHaan's view there is no such thing as an honest atheist. In fact, atheism is nothing more than a self-imposed delusion to justify one's own sin by hiding it behind a superficial veneer of unbelief. This is how DeHaan puts it:

> In my dealings with people, I do find a few honest seekers who are agnostics, though not many. *Among atheists I find no honest seekers.* The atheist, says Psalm 14:1, is a fool. He is a fool because the only one he is "faking out" is himself. Someone remains an atheist perhaps in order to believe he will not have to answer to a God who might require punishment for sin. An atheist might say, "I can't find God anywhere!" But an atheist cannot find God for the same reason that a thief cannot find a policeman. He is not truly interested in finding Him.[36]

34. On this point, see my discussion in *You're Not as Crazy as I Think*, chapter 3.

35. As an aside, it is disheartening to observe how often Christians make indefensibly sweeping statements regarding the beliefs of *all* atheists or agnostics. For example, Josh McDowell offers a rather dour view of agnosticism: "*most* agnostics do not make a real effort to know if there is a God." *A Ready Defense*, 316, emphasis added. But McDowell provides no evidence to justify his claim that most agnostics don't try to know if there is a God, thereby seeming to leave us with nothing more substantial than his personal subjective opinion.

36. DeHaan, *The God You Can Know*, 43–44, emphasis added.

There are a couple things worth highlighting in this passage. First, note that DeHaan provides two independent lines of evidence for his declaration that there are no atheists who honestly seek truth. The first line of evidence is empirical; that is, it is based on his personal observations. As he puts it, "Among atheists I find no honest seekers." It doesn't take much reflection to see that this is an enormously problematic statement. Even if DeHaan has known many atheists, and he could somehow discern that in each case the individual's atheism was intellectually dishonest, it still wouldn't follow that *all* atheists are intellectually dishonest. Personal experience with a couple dozen atheists doesn't warrant sweeping statements about every single atheist any more than personal experience with a couple dozen Christians would warrant sweeping generalizations about every single Christian.

As a result, it appears that the weight must be borne by DeHaan's second line of evidence, that which is biblically based and categorical or *a priori* (the term "*a priori*" refers to a belief that is held independently of empirical observation of the world). This evidence is rooted in DeHaan's appeal to Psalm 14:1. Since we will examine this text at some length in the next chapter, we will set aside analysis of it for now.

The second point I want to highlight is DeHaan's extremely unfavorable comparison between atheism and thievery. Think about just how striking a comparison that is. Imagine that you find your neighbor breaking into cars. "You can't do that!" you exclaim. "You need to turn yourself in to the police!" "Yeah, I know," your neighbor nods ruefully, "but I just can't seem to find them." The response is absurd, of course. Clearly the problem isn't that the fellow can't find the police precinct, it's that he doesn't *want* to find it. In short, the fellow's claim is nothing more than the lamest of excuses to justify his ongoing criminality. According to DeHaan, atheist denials of God are absurd in the same way: atheists deny knowing of God because they want to justify their ongoing unbelief and sinful lifestyle.

It is now time to turn to our next example, Ron Rhodes. Mr. Rhodes is a popular speaker, author of many books, and the president of Reasoning from the Scriptures Ministries. In his book *Answering the Objections of Atheists, Agnostics, & Skeptics,* he observes that the Supreme Court has ruled the U.S. constitution protects the right of disbelief. However, Rhodes's recognition of this right sounds rather begrudging as he adds, "My greater concern is with the divine Judge who, understandably, is much less sympathetic to the cause of atheism. Indeed, the one who denies God's existence is labeled a 'fool' (Psalm 14:1; 53:1)."[37] And what does it mean when the psalmist declares the atheist a fool? Rhodes opines, "Notice this verse is not saying that a person is a fool for denying the existence of God. Rather, he is called a fool for *saying in his heart* that there is no God. The implication is that he knows better. He *says* there is no God, despite the fact that he knows there likely is one."[38] Once again we see in Rhodes's analysis the claim that atheists really do know there is a God and are merely suppressing that knowledge. This double-minded denial will, in due course, bring the righteous condemnation of the eternal judge.

Our penultimate example is R. C. Sproul, a widely influential Reformed Christian theologian, pastor, and apologist, head of Ligonier Ministries, host of the radio program *Renewing Your Mind*, and author of more than fifty books. In the following passage Sproul explains how the foolishness of atheism is explicable in terms of immorality:

> Because of the force of general revelation, every human being knows that God exists. Atheism involves the utter denial of something that is known to be true. This is why the Bible says "The fool has said in his heart, 'There is no God'" (Psalm 14:1). To be a fool in biblical terms is not to be dim-witted or lacking in intelligence; it is to be immoral.[39]

In his commentary on the book of Romans, Sproul prefaces a discussion of Romans 1 (a key text to which we will come in the next chapter) with a jolting vignette describing the time he confronted a group of atheists over the state of their souls:

> I was invited to a university campus several years ago to speak to an atheists' club. They asked me to present the intellectual case for the existence of God. I did, and as I went through the arguments for the existence of God, I kept things on an intellectual plane. All things were safe and comfortable until I got to the end of my lecture. At that point I said, "I'm giving you arguments for the existence of God, but I feel like I'm carrying coals to Newcastle because I have to tell you that I do not have to prove to you that God exists, because I think you already know it. *Your problem is not that you do not know that God exists; your problem is that you*

---

37. Rhodes, *Answering the Objections of Atheists, Agnostics, & Skeptics*, 26.
38. Ibid., 116.
39. Sproul, *Essential Truths of the Christian Faith*, 5.

*despise the God whom you know exists. Your problem is not intel-
lectual; it is moral—you hate God.*"[40]

Whoa! Don't you wish you were in *that* audience?! On second thought,
I'm glad I wasn't. I would have found it painfully embarrassing to witness
such a spectacle. Think about it: a group of skeptics extend hospitality by
inviting a Christian into their space so that he may share his perspective,
and he returns the favor by *haranguing them*. Sproul's behavior is tantamount to wiping mud on your host's clean white carpet. Please take note
of this sorry display of Christianity when we consider in later chapters the
reasons that people become (and remain) atheists, for I suspect shameful
behavior like this is a significant factor. For now we can simply note that
Sproul's speech represents one of the boldest (and most combative) expressions of the Rebellion Thesis we have yet encountered. In his view, atheists
are engaged in a shameful charade in which they deny the obvious, spurred
on by nothing more than hatred of God.[41]

Finally, we turn to our last example: James Spiegel, Professor of Philosophy and Religion at Taylor University in Uplands, Indiana. In 2010 Professor Spiegel published *The Making of an Atheist: How Immorality Leads to
Unbelief*, an entire book devoted to analyzing the immoral foundations of
atheism. The catalyst for the book appears to be the vitriolic new atheists.
But Spiegel does not limit his critique to the so-called new atheism. Instead,
he believes the real, underlying problem is with atheism itself: In his view
the denial of God is borne of sinful rebellion. Because of this, Spiegel asserts that atheism is not a legitimate intellectual position. On the contrary,
"It is little more than moral rebellion cloaked in academic regalia. The new
atheists are blinded by their own sin."[42] Spiegel believes that atheists shirk
an "objective assessment of evidence" because of "stubborn disobedience"
and "willful rebellion."[43] "Atheism," he writes, "is the suppression of truth by

---

40. Sproul, *The Righteous Shall Live by Faith: Romans*, 40, emphasis added.

41. Even if one believes, as Sproul clearly does, that atheists really do despise God,
is this the best way to communicate that conviction? I doubt it. Had Sproul instead re-
mained on the "intellectual plane" he could have allowed the strength of his arguments
to gnaw away at the intellectual rationalizations he believes these atheists illegitimately
proffer to justify their disbelief. As it stands, he negated the value of those arguments by
turning the spotlight on his ill-begotten psychoanalysis. Now the only thing these folk
will remember is the fact that the Christian they invited returned their hospitable invitation with insults and presumptuous judgments.

42. Spiegel, *The Making of an Atheist*, 16.

43. Ibid., 18.

wickedness, the cognitive consequence of immorality. In short, it is *sin* that is the mother of unbelief."[44]

In addition to the standard appeals to Psalm 14:1 and Romans 1:18–21, Spiegel provides further scriptures as guides for analyzing the nature of atheistic rebellion. For instance, he appeals to Ephesians 4:17–19 whilst observing that "The root of the problem, apparently, is not a lack of intelligence but rather a hardness of heart that is itself caused by immoral behavior."[45] He also cites John 3:19–21, "men loved darkness instead of light because their deeds were evil," and then he observes:

> Note also Jesus' point that evildoers do not simply ignore or reject the light but actually "hate" it. If this is so, then we should expect some atheists to display a certain amount of bitterness and even rage toward the idea of God. And, of course, this is just what we find among many atheists, especially the leaders of the new atheism.[46]

To sum up, in *The Making of an Atheist* Spiegel provides one of the most comprehensive defenses of the Rebellion Thesis. Atheism, so Spiegel believes, reflects one's hatred of God and an incendiary denial of his divine sovereign rule.

Spiegel's provocative book was warmly received by many evangelical Christians. For example, philosopher and apologist Douglas Groothuis describes the book as "a clear, biblically-informed, philosophically-astute and well-documented account of the ultimate origins of atheism, which is increasingly raising its often ugly head in American and European culture."[47] Many other Christians agree with Groothuis's assessment.[48]

And that brings us to the end of our brief survey. All in all, it would appear that John Hagee and *God's Not Dead* are not leftovers from an earlier age after all. Indeed, the Rebellion Thesis continues to thrive within contemporary Christianity. And this presses the question of whether Christians can hope to defend the thesis biblically and empirically. To those questions we now turn.

---

44. Ibid.

45. Ibid., 52.

46. Ibid., 55.

47. Groothuis, Review of James Spiegel, *The Making of an Atheist*.

48. For example, see Borgman, Review of James Spiegel, *The Making of an Atheist*.

3

Does the Bible say atheists are fools?

Gavin D'Costa recalls an incident in which the Indian Christian D. T. Niles encountered the renowned theologian Karl Barth. In the exchange Barth reiterated a provocative statement that he had made often: all non-Christian religions, he insisted, represent "unbelief." D'Costa observes,

> Niles replied, asking "How many Hindus, Dr. Barth, have you met?" Barth's unhesitating reply was "Not one." To this, Niles pressed the issue a little further: "How then do you know that Hinduism is unbelief?" Barth's answer, which took Niles by surprise, was quite simply "A Priori!"[1]

As I noted in the last chapter, the term "a priori" refers to knowledge or understanding available apart from experience. Barth believed that he could know a priori without ever having met a Hindu that all Hindus are in unbelief. And he believed he was justified in making such sweeping declarations about all Hindus because his theological system entailed it. Similarly, many Christians believe they are justified in the sweeping declaration of the Rebellion Thesis because the Bible teaches it.

But *does* the Bible teach it?

It would appear that Christians widely assume that the primary evidence for the Rebellion Thesis comes from the Bible. Obviously this fact will mean little to those who reject the Bible, but for those who do accept it as God's revelation, this is very significant. Consequently, if we are to render an opinion on whether Christians ought to endorse the Rebellion

1. D'Costa, "Towards a Trinitarian Theology of Religions," 141.

Thesis, a starting point for discussion is to consider whether the Christian Bible even supports such a claim to begin with.

With this in mind, we can orient ourselves to the terrain by turning to the entry on "atheism" in *Nelson's Quick Reference Topical Bible Index*:

A. Defined as

The fool's philosophy *Ps. 14:1; Ps. 53:1*
Living without God *Rom. 1:20–32; Eph. 2:12*

B. Manifestations of, seen in:

Defiance of God *Ex. 5:2; 2 Kin. 18:19–35*
Irreligion *Titus 1:16*
Corrupt morals *Rom. 13:12–13, 1 Pe. 4:3*[2]

According to *Nelson's*, atheism is a "fool's philosophy," one which is constituted by a rejection of God that is manifested in defiance of the divine and the embrace of irreligion and corrupt morals. The entry lists the following texts as relevant to the biblical definition of atheism: Psalm 14:1, Psalm 53:1, Romans 1:20–32, and Ephesians 2:12. This is a helpful list and I will follow it in my survey, albeit with a couple changes. To begin with, given that Psalm 14 and 53 have a closely parallel structure, I will restrict the discussion to Psalm 14 so as to avoid redundancy. Further, in my treatment of Romans 1, I will focus on verses 18–21, which seem to me more directly relevant to the assessment of atheism than verses 20–32.

Psalm 14:1 (cf. Psalm 53:1)

Let's begin by considering Psalm 14:1, a text with which we are already well familiar from our survey of Christian attitudes toward atheism in chapter 2. Beginning with the "Atheist's Day" anecdote, we saw that Christians have repeatedly appealed to this verse to support the Rebellion Thesis. But is that really a correct reading? James Spiegel certainly believes so. He speaks for many when he writes:

> When smart people go in irrational directions, it is time to look elsewhere than reasoning ability for an explanation. And Scripture gives us clear direction as to where we should look. Consider the psalmist's declaration that "the fool says in his heart, 'There

2. "Atheism—The Denial of God's Existence," in *Nelson's Quick Reference Topical Bible Index*.

is no God'" (Psalm 14:1). The Hebrew term rendered "fool" here denotes a person who is "morally deficient." And elsewhere in the Old Testament Wisdom Literature we learn of various symptoms of this moral deficiency. The book of Proverbs says "a fool finds no pleasure in understanding" (Proverbs 18:2), that "fools despise wisdom and discipline" (Proverbs 1:7), that "a fool finds pleasure in evil conduct" (Proverbs 10:23) and is "hotheaded and reckless" (Proverbs 14:16).[3]

As with several other Christian writers surveyed, Spiegel simply *assumes* the text applies to atheists and he infers from this that it supports the Rebellion Thesis. But are these assumptions justified? I will argue that they are not.

Let's begin by conceding for the sake of argument (and *only* for the sake of argument) that the text *is* addressing intellectual atheists. In other words, when the psalmist speaks of the individual who "says in his heart there is no God," what he is in fact referring to is the individual who denies that God exists (i.e., the atheist). With that in mind, as we proceed we'll follow this designation: "A" = fools and "B" = atheists. On this interpretation, Psalm 14:1 reduces to the following:

$$(A) \qquad (B)$$

(1) All fools are atheists.

However, that is *not* what the Rebellion Thesis claims. In fact, on the Rebellion Thesis the order is reversed:

$$(B) \qquad (A)$$

(2) All atheists are fools.

And this is where the problem arises, for any attempt to infer (2) from (1) commits the logical fallacy of illicit conversion. To illustrate, all Ford Mustangs are cars, but it doesn't follow that all cars are Ford Mustangs. By the same token, even if (1) all fools are atheists, it doesn't follow that (2) all atheists are fools, for it may be that other atheists are *not* fools (i.e., that they are intelligent, reflective people).[4] Since the Rebellion Thesis does claim that all atheists are fools, one cannot appeal to Psalm 14:1 to justify it.

---

3. Spiegel, *The Making of an Atheist*, 51.

4. Even worse, (1) is itself false because some fools are theists. In fact, I argue below that the real force of this passage is to serve as an indictment of, and warning for, those foolish theists.

Thus far I've granted for the sake of argument that when the psalmist refers to the one who "says in his heart there is no God" we should understand that to mean "is an atheist." Even with this assumption I've demonstrated that the text does not logically support the Rebellion Thesis. Now it is time to go further and challenge the assumption itself, for I believe it to be *demonstrably false*. In order to see why, we can begin with an important hermeneutical truism: in any reading of a text, attention to context is of paramount importance. As Aaron B. Hebbard observes, with only a touch of hyperbole, "Conceivably the three most important rules in interpretation are context, context, context."[5] There are different levels of context relevant to understanding a passage, and we shall consider two here, the broader cultural context and the immediate literary/textual context.

We begin with the broader cultural backdrop (or worldview) in which this text was originally written. Our starting point is to recognize that intellectual atheism as it has been understood since the seventeenth century played *no* part in that cultural backdrop. As we saw in our survey, intellectual atheism is a phenomenon that belongs in large part to the modern world. While intellectual atheists in Europe were exceedingly rare prior to the seventeenth century, they were simply *unheard of* more than two millennia earlier in the ancient Near East (ANE) when the psalms were written.

One simple way to illumine the radical difference between the ANE and the modern West is by recognizing that ancient peoples did not maintain the distinction familiar to our age between nature (the natural world of mundane human experience and scientific enquiry) and supernature (the spiritual world of God and created spirit beings). In our modern age, we clearly distinguish these two spheres. And so today theists attempt to conceive how God and the supernatural realm interact with the natural realm while atheists aim to do away with the supernatural realm altogether.

The crucial point to appreciate is that this whole debate is a modern one and thus it was simply not on the horizon of ancient peoples. While ancient peoples recognized there were aspects of reality inaccessible to them, they didn't have a neat division between nature and supernature. Instead, they perceived reality to be a unified whole such that the natural world of daily life was freely explained in terms of the activity of divine beings. For example, natural events like floods, storms, droughts, and

---

5. In case you're wondering about the context of Hebbard's statement, see *Reading Daniel as a Text in Theological Hermeneutics*, 142.

earthquakes were all explained seamlessly as the actions of God or the gods.[6] The ANE world lacked the conceptual space to conceive the world apart from the reality of supernatural beings. Given this vast difference in worldview, it is hopelessly anachronistic to read back into Psalm 14:1 a modern atheistic position that conceptually distinguishes nature from supernature and then denies the existence of the latter.

So if the psalm is not addressing intellectual atheism, then what *is* it concerned with? At this point we can shift our attention from the ancient cultural context of Psalm 14:1 to its literary context. To get a handle on that context we will expand our view beyond verse 1 to encompass the next two verses as well:

> **1** The fool says in his heart,
>   "There is no God."
> They are corrupt, their deeds are vile;
>   there is no one who does good.
>
> **2** The LORD looks down from heaven
>   on all mankind
> to see if there are any who understand,
>   any who seek God.
> **3** All have turned away, all have become corrupt;
>   there is no one who does good,
>   not even one.

Let's begin with the relationship between the interior condition of the heart, external action, and professed belief. As a way into the discussion, let's start with the tagline that my friend includes on his email: "You show me what you mean by what you do." With that in mind, it would seem that the psalmist is arguing that our actions (what we do) provide a window into the true condition of the heart (what we think). And this often conflicts with our verbally professed belief in God (what we say). In short, our actions reveal the true state of our heart. As Jesus said: "these people honor me with their lips, but their hearts are far from me" (Matt 15:8).[7]

So how widespread is this breakdown between action, belief, and proclamation? In reality, *everybody* falls under the indictment of the passage at some point in their life. The psalmist's ultimate target is not intellectual atheists or any other subset of the human population. Instead, it is the

---

6. See Saunders, *Divine Action and Modern Science*, chapters 1, 2.

7. Thanks to Robin Parry for suggesting this verse.

whole human race. As the psalmist puts it, *all* human beings have turned away, *all* are corrupt, and *not one* does good. This bleak picture provides us with the key to what is meant in the first verse. To sum up, while everybody in the ANE professed belief in God (or gods) with his or her mouth, the psalmist observes that *nobody lived consistently with that confession.* While the entire human race may be the broader target, the immediate target in context is the community of Israel which confesses faith in Yahweh and yet fails to live up to that faith. (Covenantal faithfulness, like charity, begins at home.) Consequently, the psalmist is most immediately concerned to indict the rampant hypocrisy of those in ancient Israel who *live as if God doesn't exist, even while they profess that he does.*

Given the fact that Psalm 14:1 is so commonly used as an indictment of atheists, it is surely ironic to observe that it is, in fact, an indictment of devotees of Yahweh who fail to live up to their professed belief. Indeed, the use of this text as a proof-text to smear atheists calls to mind Jesus's strong words against the sin of (religious) hypocrisy. Consider as an example the following sober warning in Matthew 23:2–3: "The teachers of the law and the Pharisees sit in Moses's seat. So you must be careful to do everything they tell you. But do not do what they do, for they do not practice what they preach." Needless to say, it is the height of hypocrisy for religious leaders to enforce standards of observance on others that many in their own community (and perhaps they themselves) fail to maintain. To put it another way, how ironic it is that a text that was intended to warn against religious hypocrisy is instead proof-texted as a rhetorical bludgeon against atheists who make no such faith confession in the first place.

And just who is the fool exactly?

Ephesians 2:12

At this point we will briefly consider Ephesians 2:12 before turning to the most important passage of all, Romans 1:18–21. In this section of the letter, Paul is reminding the Ephesian Christians (converts from Roman paganism) about their lost state prior to conversion to Jesus the Messiah:

> remember that at that time you were separate from Christ, excluded from citizenship in Israel and foreigners to the covenants of the promise, without hope and *without God* in the world.

This passage warrants mention because it contains the single occurrence of the word "atheist" in the entire Bible. More precisely, it contains the Greek adjective *"atheos,"* which is translated "without God." So what can we learn about intellectual atheism from this passage?

The answer, it would seem, is not much. Prior to their conversion to Christianity the Ephesian Christians weren't intellectual atheists in the modern sense. Rather, they were Roman pagans who believed in many deities. According to Alan Richardson's *Dictionary of Christian Theology,*

> The Greek word "atheist" (used in the NT only at Eph. 2:12) did not mean one who denied the existence of God or the supernatural, but rather one who refused to venerate the popular civic or imperial deities and thus was suspected of political deviationism (*cf.* the case of Socrates).[8]

David Williamson and George Yancey observe that "atheos" initially appeared in ancient Greece simply as a means "to accuse and deride those without belief in the forms of religion that dominated the cultural landscape of that era."[9]

From this we can see that in the ancient Roman world the term "atheist" functioned as an epithet equivalent to calling someone a "heretic" or "apostate" or "pagan" today. This is why ancient Romans and early Christians could call each other "atheist" with no sense of irony. This phenomenon is memorably illustrated in the famous martyrdom of second-century Christian bishop Polycarp. When the proconsul demanded that Polycarp renounce the Christians by uttering the declaration "Away with the atheists!" the bishop promptly obliged . . . albeit not in the way the proconsul had anticipated. Instead, he wryly gestured toward the watching Roman crowds, looked heavenward, and intoned, "Away with the atheists!" The meaning was not lost on those gathered—Polycarp had turned the tables by flipping the atheist charge back on his persecutors—and for his bold and clever response the good bishop was promptly rewarded by being burned at the stake.[10]

---

8. Richardson, "Atheism," 18.

9. Williamson and Yancey, *There is No God: Atheists in America*, 7.

10. See "Martyrdom of Polycarp," 11. For further discussion of the perceived irreligiosity of Christians in early Roman society see Wilken, *The Christians as the Romans Saw Them*, chapter 3. David Rankin summarizes how second-century theologian and apologist Athenagoras sought to defend Christians against the charge. See *Athenagoras: Philosopher and Theologian.*

To sum up, Ephesians 2:12 reflects the first-century rhetorical usage of *atheos* as a general denunciation of those outside one's particular belief community or opposed to one's accepted orthodox confession. As such, the term shares little with the modern phenomenon of intellectual atheism that has taken hold since the Enlightenment, and so it provides no support for the Rebellion Thesis.

Romans 1:18–21

If Psalm 14:1 provides the most popular jingoistic catch-phrase to be trotted out against atheists, Romans 1:18–21 constitutes the most substantial biblical-theological case. William Lane Craig, arguably the most influential Christian apologist working today, expresses the sentiment of many when he writes: "the entire question is: are people sufficiently informed to be held morally responsible for failing to believe in God? The biblical answer to that question is unequivocal. First, God has provided a revelation of Himself in nature that is sufficiently clear for all cognitively normal persons to know that God exists."[11] Is Craig correct here? It would appear that much depends on the meaning of "cognitively normal." That is, what qualifies as "cognitively normal" and how many of us meet that standard? Those are difficult and important questions, but suffice it to say that it is one thing to claim that some atheists rebelliously suppress knowledge of God and it is quite another to claim that *all* atheists do so. If we're going to evaluate the latter claim, we should first consider Romans 1:18–21 in its entirety:

> 18 The wrath of God is being revealed from heaven against all the godlessness and wickedness of people, who suppress the truth by their wickedness, 19 since what may be known about God is plain to them, because God has made it plain to them. 20 For since the creation of the world God's invisible qualities—his eternal power and divine nature –have been clearly seen, being understood from what has been made, so that people are without excuse.
>
> 21 For although they knew God, they neither glorified him as God nor gave thanks to him, but their thinking became futile and their foolish hearts were darkened.

We can start by noting that the target in this passage is "godless and wicked" people who manifest their wickedness by suppressing a knowledge of God's divine nature, which Paul describes as being generally available

11. Craig, *A Reasonable Response*, 230.

to all people through the natural world. One can certainly see how this passage *could* be taken to support the Rebellion Thesis. But does it *really*?

Let's start by returning to the question of cultural context. Given that the concept of atheism as we understand it was not a live option in the first century it is most doubtful that Paul was thinking of atheists when he wrote derisively of godless and wicked people. Instead, it would appear much more likely that his immediate target in this passage is the pagan Gentile who ignores or suppresses their natural knowledge of God's nature in favor of idols and pagan religious practices, a target that would comport well with the usage of *atheos* in Ephesians 2:12.

Paul refers to this generally available knowledge elsewhere as well. For example, when the citizens of Lystra identify Paul and Barnabas as Hermes and Zeus, the horrified missionaries reply that God "has not left himself without testimony: he has shown kindness by giving you rain from heaven and crops in their seasons; he provides you with plenty of food and fills your hearts with joy" (Acts 14:17). In this exchange Paul and Barnabas are pointing out that the pagans should have sufficient natural knowledge of the true God to know that God is not to be confused with two frail and fallible human missionaries.

Now let's turn to the broader literary context. If Paul's immediate target in 1:18–21 is Gentile paganism, his ultimate goal in the whole sweep of Romans 1–3 is to establish the universal fallenness of *all* humanity. As F. F. Bruce explains, "Paul's aim is to show that the whole of humanity is morally bankrupt, unable to claim a favorable verdict at the judgment bar of God, desperately in need of his mercy and pardon."[12] Yes, the pagans are guilty, but only as one expression of a wider human guilt that encompasses Jew and Gentile alike. This entails that the common practice of invoking this passage as a means to single out atheists as being especially wicked and godless is really to miss the point twice over, first in terms of the immediate pagan context and second in terms of the wider focus upon universal depravity.

The second point on universal depravity becomes luminously clear in Romans 3:10–12, which consists of a quote from Psalm 14:2–3, thereby bringing us full circle back to Psalm 14 in our survey. Paul writes:

> 10 There is no one righteous, not even one;
> 11 there is no one who understands;
>   there is no one who seeks God.

12. Bruce, *Romans*, 77.

12 All have turned away,
    they have together become worthless;
there is no one who does good,
    not even one.

How ironic it is that Christian defenders of the Rebellion Thesis miss the message of Psalm 14 twice over (first in Psalm 14 itself and then again when it is repeated here in Romans 1–3), thereby missing the warning the texts present to them, and instead opting to single out contemporary atheists for special censure. I quoted Douglas Groothuis earlier as referring to the "ugly head" of atheism. Perhaps Christians ought to worry less about the ugly head of atheism and more about the ugly head of Christian hypocrisy.

While these are important caveats for any attempt to invoke Romans 1:18–21 in support of the Rebellion Thesis, the text still may provide that support. After all, as Craig observes, the text asserts that the revelation of God in nature "is sufficiently clear for all cognitively normal persons to know that God exists." Doesn't that yet provide a *de facto* indictment of atheistic unbelief? Christian philosopher James Spiegel opines:

> In this passage Paul makes clear that the problem with those who don't believe in God [be they ancient pagans or modern atheists] is not lack of evidence. On the contrary, God has made His existence and attributes so "plain" and "clearly seen" from creation that belief is inexcusable. He also explains how, in spite of this, some reject the truth, specifically through immoral behavior.[13]

With this in mind, one could concede both that the immediate target of Romans 1:18–21 is Roman paganism and that the broader target of Romans 1–3 is universal human depravity, and *still* insist that atheists too are swept up in the dragnet of the text's indictments. With that possibility in mind it would appear that this is going to require a closer look.

Let's start by considering the reference in the passage to the general availability of this knowledge of God. The Greek word translated as "plain" (*phaneros*) means "visible, clear, plainly to be seen, open, evident."[14] The idea is underscored by the second Greek word, *kathoraō* (translated as "clearly seen") which means "to see from above," "to see clearly," or "to understand." If something is clearly evident or easy to understand, then we can reasonably conclude that those who purport not to perceive or understand it are

13. Spiegel, *The Making of an Atheist*, 53.
14. Dunn, *Romans 1–8*, 56.

either cognitively deficient (e.g., blind, deaf, or mentally incapacitated) or they are stubbornly suppressing or otherwise refusing to acknowledge that which they do understand. Since atheists are not cognitively deficient, we seem constrained to conclude that their unbelief falls into the latter category. And so, it looks like the Rebellion Thesis might find indirect support from Romans 1:18–21 after all.

At this point an analogy might be helpful to illumine the nature of the suppression of knowledge that is being alleged. I provide the following illustration in my book *You're not as Crazy as I Think*:

> Imagine that you're walking in the woods with a friend one dark night when you suddenly hear a roar in the darkness. "Did you hear that?" you cry to your friend, but he shakes his head and looks at you strangely. Moments later you see a light flash just over the crest of the hill so bright that it illumines the surrounding forest with the brilliance of the noonday sun. "Did you see that?" you whisper in awe to your friend. But he throws another strange look your way and shakes his head. A second later the ground beneath you shudders from a massive impact. "Did you feel that?" you shout out to your friend, but he just stares blankly back at you as if you're crazy. What would you think of your friend's reaction (or lack thereof) to this succession of stupendous sensory stimuli? Either he is for some reason unable to sense these phenomena or else he did sense them but for some reason—mischievousness? stubbornness?—he refuses to acknowledge them.[15]

Assuming that the individual's cognitive faculties are working properly, we would have to conclude that he really did see, hear, and feel something and was simply refusing to acknowledge those experiences. It would seem that Romans 1 leaves us with an analogous picture of the atheist as one who really does "see, hear, and feel" the presence of God, and yet sinfully denies it. As a result, even if we must admit the irrelevance of Psalm 14:1 to the question, one might conclude that Romans 1 alone is sufficient to establish the Rebellion Thesis.

However, before the Christian triumphantly reinstates the Rebellion Thesis, I would warn them against the unforeseen implications of doing so. What do I mean? Well, have you ever watched a television show or movie where one person is about to lower the boom on his or her nemesis? And then at the last moment the nemesis warns: "I wouldn't do that if I were you!" You know what that means, right? It means that the fellow who

---

15. Rauser, *You're Not as Crazy as I Think*, 189.

thinks he's about to nail his nemesis is unwittingly stepping into a trap and if he proceeds he'll end up taking himself down in the process. It seems to me that this is the very situation the Christian faces at present. And so, to the folks determined to find the seeds of the Rebellion Thesis in Romans 1:18–21 I say, I wouldn't do that if I were you!

Okay, that's enough by way of dramatic setup. You're probably wondering why I wouldn't do that, so let me explain. I will do so in two steps, beginning with the impact that this position has on agnosticism. The problem here is that if the existence and nature of God really are always plain (*phaneros*) and clear (*kathoraō*) to all people all the time then it isn't just atheists who are impugned for their disbelief: the *same* goes for *any and every agnostic*.

This is an interesting consequence, particularly given that Christians have often taken a more sympathetic view of agnosticism. For example, in our survey of historical and contemporary attitudes toward atheism in chapter 2, I noted that Dan DeHaan acknowledges that he has met honest agnostics, even though he has never met an honest atheist. But if God's existence and nature are always plain and clear then the agnostic is as bereft of excuses as the atheist. Think again of the illustration where one's companion claims not to see, hear, or feel the stupendous explosion in the woods. Imagine that instead of declaring he had heard, seen, and felt *nothing* (an analogy with the atheist) the bloke claimed that he *didn't believe* he had heard, seen, or felt anything, *nor did he believe he hadn't*. This would make him precisely parallel with the agnostic, as one without belief either way. Assuming that the man was functioning properly (and thus not cognitively deficient), one would likely conclude that he was being disingenuous: perhaps he was being deceptive or stubbornly refusing to acknowledge what he'd experienced for some reason. Whatever the case might be, the proper conclusion would be that *the agnostic is every bit as culpable as the atheist*. If the existence and nature of God are plain and clear to the atheist then they are also plain and clear to the agnostic, period. And so if there are no honest atheists, neither are there any honest agnostics.

That's bad. But it's about to get worse. A lot worse.

The next problem is that the same implications that take down the honest agnostic likewise take down the honest Christian doubter. If God's existence and nature really are plain and clear to all then it follows that any doubt a Christian might have about God's existence and/or nature constitutes sinful rebellion as surely as does that of the atheist and agnostic. But

43

surely that *can't* be right. Many Christians find that at some point in their Christian walk they are on similar ground as the agnostic, wracked with doubts and unsure about what they believe: "Lord I believe!" they pray, "*Help my unbelief!*" Doubts are so common in the Christian life that John Bunyan includes them in his beloved allegory of the Christian journey, *Pilgrim's Progress,* with the image of "Doubting Castle," a forlorn place that temporarily holds the protagonist Christian in its bleak confines. Bunyan includes Doubting Castle for good reason, as many Christians find themselves sojourning in its dark and drafty halls. During this time they may question the goodness, wisdom, or even the very existence of God.

By the way, Christian doubters are not limited to those spiritually nebulous folks who sit in the back pew every Sunday. Some of these doubters have been very high profile Christians with unparalleled reputations of holiness and saintliness. Just consider the case of that modern saint and servant to the world's poor, Mother Teresa. A few years after she passed away, Mother Teresa's journals were published and they revealed a soul that was often tortured and beset with doubts and questions. For example, she wrote,

> They say people in hell suffer eternal pain because of the loss of God—they would go through all that suffering if they had just a little hope of possessing God.—In my soul I feel just that terrible pain of loss—of God not wanting me—of God not being God—of God not really existing (Jesus, please forgive my blasphemies—I have been told to write everything). That darkness that surrounds me on all sides—I can't lift my soul to God—no light or inspiration enters my soul. I speak of love for souls—of tender love for God—words pass through my words [*sic,* lips]—and I long with a deep longing to believe in them.—What do I labour for? If there be no God—there can be no soul. If there is no soul then Jesus—You also are not true.—Heaven, what emptiness—not a single thought of Heaven enters my mind—for there is no hope.[16]

In this remarkably candid passage, Mother Teresa admits that she struggles with all manner of doubts, to the point of even questioning whether God exists and whether Jesus is a real savior. And she's not alone: countless Christians can resonate deeply with this honest account of struggle. This reminds us yet again that doubt is indeed a standard part of the Christian life. The fact is that God's existence and nature do not always

16. Mother Teresa, *Come be My Light,* 192–93.

appear plain and clear, even to very saintly people. Surely that much *is* plain and clear.

And so I say to the Christian, *that's* why I wouldn't do that if I were you. Insisting that Romans 1:18–21 grounds the Rebellion Thesis leaves the Christian with a real dilemma. If they insist on pressing the Pauline text into service to condemn atheists based on the plain and clear witness to the existence and nature of God, they likewise indict agnostics and even *every Christian who ever harbors a doubt about God's existence or nature.* Consequently, the dragnet of Romans 1 sweeps up the doubts of Mother Teresa, treating those doubts as every bit as rebellious and wicked as those of infamous atheist activist Madalyn Murray O'Hair. And that brings us to the bottom line: if the Christian can't accept the conclusion that Mother Teresa was sinfully suppressing the plain and clear witness of creation to the existence and nature of God, then he or she is obliged to reject the Rebellion Thesis reading of Romans 1.

In conclusion, it seems to me that the implications of the Rebellion Thesis are simply intolerable. The Christian cannot deny the fact that God's existence and nature are *not* always plain and clear. The fact is that there are countless people of religious faith who have *not* always found God's existence and nature to be plain and clear. Think, for example, of those who survived the gas chambers of the concentration camps or the blood soaked fields of Rwanda. The same might be said of a couple who discover that their young son has terminal cancer, or that their daughter was raped by the beloved family priest. (We'll return to the second example in chapter 5.) Sometimes God's existence and nature are plain and clear to us, and those are wonderful moments that can give us strength for the journey. But at other times we may not know which way is up and which is down, our prayers may not seem to go above the ceiling and we may even struggle to take our next breath. That is an undeniable aspect of the Christian life and if you find yourself walking through that valley of despair it does not mean you are in sinful rebellion. Nor need it indicate any other kind of personal failure: It's simply the reality of life in a broken world. That which is true of the Christian may be equally true of the agnostic or atheist.

I'm going to make one final point with respect to this whole picture before we wrap this chapter up. It must be said that treating all doubt as sinful rebellion has the uncomfortable whiff of word of faith theology about it. According to word of faith theology, any illness of the body is indicative of a lack of faith in the person. On the perspective of this theology, if you're sick then ultimately it's *your fault*. I mentioned in the previous paragraph the example of a child who has terminal cancer. According to word of faith theology, if that child is not healed it is the result of a lack of faith, either in the child himself or (perhaps) in his caregivers. But in my opinion that is an unimaginably harmful (and plainly false) view of illness. New Testament scholar Gordon Fee rightly decried this theology as a "disease" for criminalizing sickness and tainting those afflicted with it.[17] Here's the lesson for us: if it is wrong to criminalize the child's cancer, it is likewise wrong to criminalize the parents' doubts about God that might result from it.

To sum up, in this chapter we have been focused on evaluating the biblical case for the Rebellion Thesis. We quickly determined that Psalm 14:1 and Ephesians 2:12 had nothing to do with intellectual atheism and thus they could readily be set aside. However, this analysis did have one substantial payoff: it demonstrated the sobering (and deeply ironic) way that Psalm 14:1 has repeatedly been proof-texted as a condemnation of atheism. As we saw, this amounts to an egregious abuse of the text, which constitutes a neglect of the very warning this passage presents to the pious. The case of Romans 1:18–21 was more complex, and it must be admitted that it is indeed *possible* to read the passage as providing a sweeping indictment that includes the disbelief of the intellectual atheist. However, I pointed out that this interpretation faces significant obstacles since it requires us to view all doubt of God's existence and/or nature, even that of the struggling Christian, as manifesting immoral rebellion. In order to address this problem, I proposed a treatment of the text that moves beyond exegesis by reading the text in light of the broader biblical canon and the exigencies of lived human experience. Lest you think one ought not move beyond exegesis, keep in mind that the reader who interprets this passage against atheists is also going beyond Paul's words since the apostle clearly never had contemporary atheism in mind. So while you can try to retain a biblical basis for the Rebellion Thesis, consider this fair warning: I wouldn't do that if I were you.

17. See Fee, *The Disease of the Health and Wealth Gospels*.

4

Do atheists have an axe to grind?

Given the weakness of the biblical case for the Rebellion Thesis, we turn now to consider the empirical evidence. Does the evidence support the conclusion that most atheists demonstrate hostility toward God? Note, by the way, that I said "most." In point of fact, the thesis claims that *all* atheists are hostile, but it is certainly possible that some atheists may be adept at suppressing that hostility. As a result, the thesis can accommodate the occasional behavioral exception to the rule (i.e., an atheist who evinces no *apparent* hostility). At the same time, if we are to accept the thesis based on empirical evidence of rebellious and hostile atheists, then we should be able to identify in atheists a general pattern of hostility toward God. Is that what we do find? Do we find that atheists are generally hostile toward God?

So far as I can see, the empirical evidence that Christians proffer in support of the thesis is surprisingly flimsy and consists of a mixture of anecdotes of particular atheists (think, for example, of Addison's cowardly atheist) along with general impressions and sweeping claims (recall De-Haan's claim that he never met an honest atheist). However, testimony of this kind is simply too weak to constitute good evidence for the thesis. The fact is that it is far more difficult to identify bona fide instances of rebellious unbelief than most Christians recognize, let alone a sufficient sampling of such cases to justify the Rebellion Thesis on empirical grounds.

Let's say a bit more about that difficulty. We can begin by pointing out that even if you find a case of an individual who appears to be hostile toward God, that is not yet sufficient to provide evidence for the thesis. The problem is that it is one thing to identify hostility and it is another thing to identify *the source or catalyst* of that hostility. After all, there could be many catalysts for hostility against God, not least of which is experience with Christians behaving badly. How much ill will might be generated by the impact of an inept Christian pastor, an overbearing Christian parent, an abusive Christian friend, or some other deeply flawed ambassador of the kingdom?

We can bring the point home by considering a real life case. So consider the testimony of Emma Tom, an avowed atheist who talks candidly about the genesis of her unbelief in the essay "Confessions of a Kindergarten Leper." Tom recalls that when she was a six year old, her public school teacher told her class that children who didn't believe in God would get leprosy. Tom's parents were atheists and she was horrified to learn that her family would be stricken with the dreaded disease unless they (and she) believed in God. What a terrifying experience that would have been for a small child. And it clearly left an indelible, and very painful, mark on Tom's life. Now as she reflects on this experience, her rage is palpable: "How dare this devout bitch try to scare the bejesus into little kiddies with her tales of disease and abductions? . . . I responded by embracing fundamentalist atheism, convinced that the broad church of utter disbelief represented true tolerance and enlightenment."[1] It certainly appears that much of Tom's evident hostility is driven by her bitter experience with that abusive teacher rather than a direct, incendiary rejection of God. And that leads one to ask: how many other atheists bear hostility because of Christians behaving badly?

But what if a person expresses their hostility toward God rather than poorly behaved Christians? For example, imagine an atheist who simply declares, "If God exists then I want nothing to do with him!" That seems pretty clear. So would *that* constitute evidence for the Rebellion Thesis? The short answer is, no. Remember that according to the Rebellion Thesis it is not merely that the atheist is hostile toward God. In addition, it would have to be the case that this hostility is borne of a *hatred* of God and a *desire to sin* with impunity. Consequently, until we know that the hostility is driven by a hatred of God and a desire to sin, we are not yet in a place to conclude that the hostility presents evidence for the Rebellion Thesis. In other words, mere hostility is not enough. If we want real empirical support for the thesis

---

1. Tom, "Confessions of a Kindergarten Leper," in Blackford and Schüklenk, *50 Voices of Disbelief*, 78.

then we must be able to trace the genesis of that hostility to hatred for God and a desire to sin.

The nature of this problem becomes clear when we consider specific instances of atheistic hostility. Later in chapter 5 I will introduce you to the case of Bob Jyono, a devout Catholic who became an atheist only after discovering that his daughter had been repeatedly raped by a priest. It seems quite evident that Mr. Jyono has a great deal of divinely-directed hostility. In short, he appears to be *angry* at God, and I can't say that I blame him. Interestingly, you can find people in the Bible getting angry with God too. Just consider, for example, the psalmist in Psalm 94. But even though the psalmist is angry, this anger isn't sourced in hatred of God and a desire to sin. Rather, it is rooted in the pain of unjust suffering. And when I consider the horrific evil to which Mr. Jyono's daughter was subjected, I conclude that his anger looks much like the psalmist's. That is, it appears to be borne of the unimaginable pain of a man who reads God's perceived complicity in his daughter's rape as the ultimate act of betrayal. It's an anger borne by the injustice of the world, not a desire to sin with impunity. Perhaps that constitutes a rebellious desire to sin, but it is very far from *obvious* that it does so. And thus, Jyono's atheism doesn't provide evidence for the Rebellion Thesis.

Together these points demonstrate that it is extremely difficult to marshal empirical evidence that supports the specific claims of the Rebellion Thesis. Indeed, it appears to me that defending the thesis empirically is nearly a hopeless task. By contrast, as the Jyono case illustrates, providing putative evidence against the thesis is relatively straightforward.

To say a bit more about this, we can start with the epistemic principle of credulity. Since the philosopher Richard Swinburne is well known for defending this principle, we'll borrow his definition:

> I suggest that it is a principle of rationality that (in the absence of special considerations), if it seems (epistemically) to a subject that *x* is present (and has that characteristic), then probably *x* is present (and has that characteristic); what one seems to perceive is probably so.[2]

The point of this principle is to establish that unless you have reason to doubt your experience (e.g., sense perception, memory), it is reasonable to accept it. If it seems to you, for example, that you are awake, and you have

---

2. Swinburne, *The Existence of God,* 303.

no defeaters to the belief that you are awake, then it is reasonable to conclude that you are awake. Swinburne argues that the principle of credulity is supplemented by a broader principle of testimony according to which "Other things being equal, we believe that what others tell us that they perceived probably happened."[3] If you have no reason to doubt a person's testimony, it is reasonable to accept it. In other words, such testimony is treated as innocent until proven guilty. Within our present context this means that if atheists provide testimony as to the nature of their own unbelief which contradicts the Rebellion Thesis, and we have no independent defeaters (e.g., biblical evidence) to doubt that testimony, then it is reasonable to take that testimony as evidence against the Rebellion Thesis.

In support of the appropriateness of accepting an atheist's testimony at face value, it is also worthwhile to remember the Golden Rule: do unto others as you'd have them do unto you. Translated into our present context the maxim looks like this: if you are a Christian you wouldn't appreciate people insisting that deep down you're an atheist and that you're suppressing your latent atheistic belief. Instead, you'd expect your interlocutors to do you the minimal courtesy of taking you at your word. Christian apologist Ravi Zacharias made a relevant observation along these lines when he wrote: "Bertrand Russell's assertion, in his conceptual critique of Christianity, that all religion is born out of fear, is a weak and unthinking criticism of the subject. *It is no more true than if one were to say that all irreligion is born out of fearfulness.*"[4] Zacharias is right. It's simply unfair to dismiss religion as arising from fear just as it is unfair to dismiss atheism (or irreligion) as arising from fear. I'd simply add that it is likewise unfair to dismiss an atheist's testimony as arising from the suppression of latent theistic belief.

With that in mind, if we want to subject the Rebellion Thesis to further scrutiny, it would seem reasonable to do so by way of carefully considering the testimony of an atheist as to the nature and grounds of their own unbelief. To that end, I have invited atheist Jeffery Jay Lowder to share with us his own commitment to atheism. Jeff certainly comes well equipped for the task. As I noted in chapter 1, way back in 1995 at the dawn of the internet Jeff co-founded Internet Infidels, a major internet hub for skeptical and atheistic discourse.[5] Over the last twenty years Jeff has continued to be a vocal proponent for atheism, including co-editing a book critiquing

3. Ibid., 322.

4. Zacharias, *The Real Face of Atheism*, 21–22.

5. http://www.patheos.com/blogs/secularoutpost/about-us/

the resurrection,[6] engaging in public debates on the existence of God,[7] and blogging.[8] I selected Jeff as an interlocutor not only because he is well credentialed, but also because he strikes me as an amiable and laidback fellow with no particular axe to grind against theism. In short, Jeff doesn't *seem* to be in rebellion.

So here's the plan. I'm going to ask Jeff to explain his atheistic views and why he holds them. Along the way, we will be looking to see whether Jeff can articulate his position with reason and without discernable hostility toward God. Insofar as our conversation fails to provide evidence of God-directed hostility, it will constitute additional empirical evidence against the Rebellion Thesis.

And so, without further ado, let's now turn to our conversation. Please note that this dialogue unfolded via emails over several weeks. In the dialogue I am designated as "RR" and Jeff is "JL" (though you probably would have guessed that anyway). Also note that the footnotes accompanying Jeff's comments are also written by Jeff.

A conversation with atheist Jeff Lowder

RR: Jeff, thanks for joining us for a discussion on atheism. Let's begin with definitions. What is an atheist?

JL: Thanks, Randal. Your question is a great one to start with. Your readers might be surprised to learn that, among people who self-identify as an atheist, there are many opinions about the "correct" definition of "atheism." There are many self-described atheists who define atheism as the "mere lack of belief that God exists," while there are others who define atheism as a *belief*—the belief that God does not exist. There are other approaches as well. I, for one, fall into the second group and so I define an atheist as a person who believes that God does not exist.[9]

6. Lowder and Price, eds. *The Empty Tomb: Jesus Beyond the Grave.*

7. You can watch Lowder's debate with Christian apologist Phil Fernandes at Exposed Atheists, "Naturalism vs. Theism: Jeffrey Jay Lowder vs. Phil Fernandes."

8. Lowder currently blogs at "The Secular Outpost," http://www.patheos.com/blogs/secularoutpost/.

9. At the risk of belaboring the point, I want to remind our nontheistic readers that Randal and I are stipulating a definition of "atheism." We agree that "atheist" refers to a person who believes that God does not exist. If any of our nontheistic readers strongly disagree with that definition, rather than try to persuade them to adopt our definition, I

Since that definition includes the word "God," the full definition of atheism depends upon the definition of God. How do you define God?

RR: It is generally recognized that Western monotheisms—Judaism, Christianity, and Islam—share a common understanding of God, which is called "classical theism." According to that definition, as I understand it, God is a necessary agent who is omnipotent, omniscient, omnipresent, and perfectly good (or omnibenevolent), and the creator of the universe. As a theist, I believe God, so defined, exists, while you deny that God exists.

Now you've been active in the atheist community for many years, so I take it you have a good read on why people purport to be atheists. Could you provide a quick overview of some of the reasons people provide for disbelief?

JL: Imagine we did an opinion poll of atheists and verified that all of the respondents really do believe there is no God. Suppose we then asked them, "Why do you believe that?" I think the majority of those atheists would give one or more of the following reasons: (1) pain and suffering; (2) the reasonableness of nonbelief in God (aka "divine hiddenness"); (3) religious confusion among believers; (4) the irrelevance of God to science; (5) one or more contradictions in the definition of God; and (6) the lack of evidence for God's existence.

RR: Which of those reasons for atheism do you find to be most intellectually persuasive?

JL: I think (1) and (2) are the strongest of those six reasons for atheism, but, as a group, I don't think those six reasons are the best reasons to be an atheist. In my opinion, the best reasons to be an atheist are the best reasons to be a metaphysical naturalist. Allow me to explain.

(Metaphysical) supernaturalism is the hypothesis that one or more nonphysical mental entities created the physical world. (Metaphysical) naturalism is the hypothesis that the universe is a closed system, which means that nothing that is not part of the natural world affects it.[10]

---

would simply ask them to pretend that we are speaking a foreign language. Our language looks and sounds just like English, with the sole exception that we are using the word "atheist" as defined above. The point is that it's not helpful to get hung up on semantics here. Whether you call it "atheism" or "schmatheism," the *belief represented by the word* is what we want to discuss.

10. Draper, "Seeking But Not Believing," 198.

Naturalism has two consequences. First, naturalism entails that, if there is such a thing as a mental world, the physical world explains why there is anything mental at all.[11] Second, naturalism entails that all forms of super-naturalism, including theism, are false.

With those preliminary matters out of the way, here are three reasons for believing that naturalism is more probable than theism.

1. Naturalism Is a Simpler Explanation than Theism.

Naturalism and supernaturalism are *symmetric* claims: the former claims that the physical explains the mental, while the latter claims that the mental explains the physical.[12] Prior to examining the evidence, both positions are equally likely to be true.

But now compare and contrast naturalism and theism. Theism says everything that supernaturalism says, but adds on several additional claims: (a) that the non-physical mental entity which explains the natural world is a *person;* (b) that person created the world *for a purpose;* and (c) that person is *omnipotent, omniscient, and omnibenevolent.*[13] Because theism entails supernaturalism but could be false even if supernaturalism is true, then, *prior to examining the evidence,* theism is less likely to be true than supernaturalism (and hence naturalism).

2. Naturalism is a More Accurate Explanation than Theism for Many Facts.

(1) Naturalism is the best explanation for the fact that all life, including conscious life, evolved from a common ancestor[14]

To be sure, biological evolution is logically compatible with theism; God *could* have used evolution to create life. But God could have *also* used many other methods to create life, methods which are impossible if naturalism is true. In contrast, if naturalism is true, evolution pretty much *has* to be true. Furthermore, since theism entails that a mind created the entire physical

---

11. In contrast, supernaturalism entails that, if there is such a thing as a physical world, the mental world explains why there is anything physical at all. See Draper, "God and Evil," 10.

12. Draper, "God and Evil," 10.

13. Ibid., 11.

14. See Draper, "Evolution and the Problem of Evil"; cf. Pojman, *Philosophy of Religion*, chapter 6.

world, theism leads us to expect that minds are fundamentally nonphysical entities and therefore that conscious life is fundamentally different from non-conscious life. But this in turn would lead us to expect that conscious life was created independently of nonconscious life—that evolution is false. Thus, the scientific fact of biological evolution is more likely on the assumption that naturalism is true than on the assumption that theism is true.

(2) Naturalism is the best explanation for the fact that human minds are dependent upon the physical brain[15]

Scientific evidence shows that human consciousness is highly dependent upon the brain.[16] In this context, nothing mental happens without something physical happening. That strongly implies that the mind cannot exist inde-pendently of physical arrangements of matter. In other words, we do not have a soul. And this is exactly what we would expect if naturalism is true. But if theism is true, then souls or, more generally, minds that do not depend on physical brains, are a real possibility. Also, theism entails the existence of at least one unembodied mind, God. (God's mind is not in any sense dependent on physical arrangements of matter.) But if nothing mental happens without something physical happening, then that is evidence against the existence of any being who is supposed to have an unembodied mind, including God. Therefore, the physical nature of minds is evidence favoring naturalism over theism.

(3) Naturalism is the best explanation for the neurological basis of moral handicaps

In many cases, our ability to choose to do morally good actions depends upon our having properly functional emotional capacities, especially *empathy* (i.e., our ability to identify what someone else is thinking or feeling and to re-spond to their thoughts and feelings with an appropriate emotion).[17] We now know, thanks to the relatively new discipline of neuroscience, that certain brain abnormalities cause people to experience less or even no empathy.[18]

15. Jeffery Jay Lowder, "The Evidential Argument from Physical Minds."
16. Tooley, "Dr. Tooley's Opening Statement."
17. Baron-Cohen, *The Science of Evil*, 16.
18. Ibid., 39.

For example, violent psychopaths may know in some abstract sense that their behavior is morally wrong, but utterly lack the *affective* capacity for empathy that enables them to understand the impact of their actions on others' feelings.[19]

While theism is compatible with a neurological basis for moral handicaps, the fact that at least some moral handicaps can be explained neurologically is more probable on naturalism than on theism. If theism is true, then that means *both*

> a) God creates some human beings with moral handicaps that are not the result of the freely chosen actions of any human being;

and

> b) These moral handicaps make it *more* likely that they will harm others.

What moral justification would God have for allowing both (a) and (b) to obtain? This seems completely random from a theistic, moral point of view, but precisely what we would expect on naturalism (and blind nature is indifferent to the moral consequences of brain abnormalities).[20]

(4) Naturalism is the best explanation for the biological role (and moral randomness) of pain and pleasure[21]

Physical pain and pleasure are systematically connected to survival and reproduction. This fact is much more probable on naturalism than it is on theism, even if we compare evolutionary naturalism to evolutionary theism (i.e., the belief that God used evolution). On the assumption that evolutionary naturalism is true (and all living things are the result of blind nature), we would expect that pain and pleasure, just like any other biological system produced by natural selection, would be fundamentally *biological* phenomena. On the

---

19. As Baron-Cohen points out, the neurological basis for moral handicaps challenges traditional views about moral responsibility. "If zero degrees of empathy is really a form of neurological disability, to what extent can such an individual who commits a crime be held responsible for what they have done? This gets tangled up with the free will debate, for if zero degrees of empathy leaves an individual to some extent 'blind' to the impact of their actions on others' feelings, then surely they deserve our sympathy rather than punishment." See *The Science of Evil*, 160.

20. Some theists have pointed out that *moral evil*, such as fallen angels or demons choosing to do evil, might explain so-called "natural evils." This argument makes the inverse point: certain natural evils explain at least some moral evil.

21. Draper, "Pain and Pleasure."

assumption that evolutionary theism is true, however, we would expect God to produce pain and pleasure only when he had morally sufficient reasons to do so. So evolutionary theism leads us to expect that pain and pleasure are fundamentally *moral* phenomena, *which just happens to be connected to the biological goals of survival and reproduction.* That's a huge coincidence that naturalism doesn't need.

It gets worse. Some pain (like the suffering endured by people with terminal illnesses or injuries) and some pleasure (like the sexual pleasure enjoyed by infertile couples, including but not limited to homosexuals) is biologically *gratuitous*—it does not contribute to survival or reproduction. On the assumption that evolutionary naturalism is true, this is just what we would expect: blind nature has no way to "fine-tune" organic systems to prevent such pain and pleasure. On evolutionary theism, however, this is extremely surprising. So biologically gratuitous pain and pleasure is very much more probable on naturalism than on theism.

(5) Naturalism is the best explanation for nonresistant nonbelief (in God)[22]

There are people who do not believe that God exists.[23] At least some of those people are "nonresistant" nonbelievers—that is, their nonbelief is "not in any way the result of their own emotional or behavioral opposition towards God or relationship with God or any of the apparent implications of such a relationship."[24] Such nonbelievers are open to having a relationship with God—in fact, they may even *desire* it—but are unable to have such a relationship.

Given that human beings exist, the fact that some of them are nonresistant nonbelievers is much more probable on the assumption that naturalism is true (and blind nature is indifferent to religious belief) than on the assumption that theism is true (and there exists a *perfectly loving* God who would ensure that a meaningful relationship was always available to those he loves).

22. Schellenberg, *Divine Hiddenness and Human Reason*; Schellenberg, *The Wisdom to Doubt*.

23. This sentence, of course, assumes that at least some (if not most) professions of atheism are genuine. Those familiar with intra-Christian debates on apologetic methodologies will notice that I have just ruled out the claim of some (or all?) presuppositionalists, namely, that there are no atheists and instead there are only *professed* atheists. I agree with John Schellenberg: "it would take something like willful blindness to fail to affirm that not all nonbelief is the product of willful blindness (even if some of it is)." See Schellenberg, "What Divine Hiddenness Reveals."

24. Schellenberg, "What Divine Hiddenness Reveals."

(6) Naturalism is the best explanation for biologically-based nonbelief.

In addition to the *general* fact of nonresistant nonbelief, there are many additional arguments for naturalism based upon very *specific* facts about nonresistant nonbelief. Here I will mention just one: individuals with Autism Spectrum Disorders (ASDs) are much more likely to be nontheists than are neurotypical individuals.[25] Furthermore, even when people with ASDs are theists, for them "God is more a principle than a person. He/it provides order but isn't much concerned with human affairs—the idea of him satisfies the intellect rather than the emotions."[26]

Individuals with ASDs have brains which excel at *systemizing,* the ability to analyze changing patterns and to figure out how things work. Those skills come at a cost, however. As Simon Baron-Cohen explains, "The downside of remarkable systemizing is a lack of interest in unlawful phenomena, the clearest case of which is emotions."[27] The result is that people with ASDs are *mindblind:* They are, to varying degrees, unable to attribute mental states to themselves and to others.[28] In extreme cases, persons with autism struggle to even *recognize* other minds besides their own. Although ASDs are complex and not fully understood, it is clear that ASDs are the result of physical differences in the brains of individuals with autism.[29]

The connection between nontheism and autism is more likely on naturalism (and nature is blind to the nontheistic tendencies of autistic brains) than it is on theism.[30]

3. Theism's Accuracy Doesn't (Seem to) Outweigh Naturalism's Accuracy.

Of course, theists can and do argue that many facts favor theism over naturalism, including the beginning of the universe, the life-permitting

25. Caldwell-Harris and McNamara, "Religious Belief Systems of Persons with High Functioning Autism." Cf. Draper, "God and Evil," 23–24; Schloss and Murray, eds., *The Believing Primate*; and Barrett, *Why Would Anyone Believe in God?*

26. Hutson, "Does Autism Lead to Atheism?"

27. Baron-Cohen, *The Science of Evil*, 117–18.

28. Baron-Cohen, *Mindblindness.*

29. Baron-Cohen, *The Science of Evil*, 99–103.

30. Incidentally, the systemizing tendencies of autistic brains also provide some evidence against the worry that atheists are "less moral" than theists. As Baron-Cohen notes, because people with ASDs tend to develop their moral codes through systemizing rather than through empathy, they tend to be "supermoral rather than immoral." See Baron-Cohen, *The Science of Evil*, 95, 121–22.

conditions of the universe, the origin of biological information, consciousness, objective moral values, moral agency, religious experience, and so forth. For the sake of argument, let's assume that all of these theistic facts really are evidence favoring theism. Even so, it seems that the theist's facts don't outweigh the naturalist's facts. (At the very least, it's far from obvious that they do.) In other words, the available evidence does not unambiguously favor theism over naturalism.

RR: Jeff, thanks for this comprehensive and articulate response! It's very helpful. You certainly seem to have some good reasons for being an atheist. I'd love to debate some of these points, but I'm going to restrain myself because my goal in this conversation isn't simply to assay the quality of the reasons you provide for being an atheist. Instead, I'd like to step behind those reasons.

Your comprehensive case is, at first blush, an impressive one. But regardless of how strong your arguments for atheism (and naturalism) may appear to be, many Christians will interpret your presentation as nothing more than very complicated, ad hoc rationalizations that you construct to justify your disbelief. The real reason for your disbelief, so they say, is not based on argument and evidence at all. Rather, it is (how can I put this delicately?) . . . sin. According to this view, you really do believe in God at some level, but you suppress that belief and mask it with these elaborate arguments of yours. In short, these arguments merely serve to justify your atheism so that you may live as if God didn't exist.

I call this interpretation of atheism the "Rebellion Thesis." I am guessing you will not be sympathetic with this dismissal of your case as a veiled attempt to deny your knowledge of God so that you may sin with impunity. However, I am interested to hear whether you've encountered this interpretation of atheism before. And I would be interested to hear your most charitable reflections on the thesis. Do you think it is possible that your atheism is due, in whole or in part, to sinful rebellion? Do you think it is possible, or perhaps even plausible, to think that some (if not all) atheism might be attributable to such factors?

Okay, let me just lay it on the line. Jeff, do you think you might hate God, and not want him to exist?

JL: Yes, I am very familiar with this interpretation of atheism. In fact, I've lost count of the number of times that some stranger, upon learning that I am an atheist, has assumed that the Rebellion Thesis is true. In response, I always point out that it's hard to hate someone (or Someone) you think doesn't exist. I, for one, have no idea how that is supposed to work: how would anyone generate emotional outrage towards a *non-existent* person? So, no, I don't think my atheism is due to hating God any more than my a-Superman-ism is due to hating Superman.

Perhaps the most plausible version of the Rebellion Thesis doesn't entail that atheists literally *hate* God; instead, it simply denies that professions of atheism are sincere or genuine. Probably the best evidences for the Rebellion Thesis are quotations from atheists (such as Thomas Nagel) who appear to hope that theism is false. As evidence goes, however, such quotations don't add much to the case for the Rebellion Thesis.

Why? The most charitable interpretation of such quotations is that they are support for a type of inductive argument known as the *Statistical Syllogism,* an argument that moves from a proposition about a population to a proposition about a sample. Statistical Syllogisms have the following form.

Z percent of F are G.
x is F.
Things that are F bear such-and-such relevance to property G.
Therefore, x is G.

Applied to the Rebellion Thesis, we get the following argument.

Many atheists admit that they want theism to be false.
John Doe is an atheist.
Therefore, John Doe wants theism to be false.

The problem with this argument is that it violates the *Rule of Total Evidence,* which is the requirement that the premises of an inductively correct argument must represent *all* of the available relevant evidence. This Statistical Syllogism ignores the evidence from the testimony of other atheists, including myself, who say that they wish that theism were true. (More on that in a moment.) If John Doe's atheism were the only thing we could know about John Doe, then this argument might be a good (inductive) argument for believing that John Doe wants theism to be false (if the first premise were true). But, assuming John Doe is a living person, the polite thing to do would be to ask John Doe what he wants, not make assumptions. (Just as atheists shouldn't assume from the outset that all theists are theists because they want theism to be true.)

Another major problem with this argument is this: even if John turns out to be one of those atheists who does not want theism to be true, that would not make his reasons for atheism weak. He may in fact have strong reasons for thinking that God does not exist. He may have very weak reasons for thinking that. He may have no reasons at all. The fact, if it is a fact, that John wants theism to be false tells us *nothing* about the existence or quality of his reasons for thinking that theism is false.

Consider an analogy. Many theists want theism to be true (i.e., they want God to exist). However, that tells us *nothing* about the existence of God or the quality of their reasons for thinking that God exists. They could have strong reasons for thinking that God exists. They may have very weak reasons for thinking that God exists. Or they may have no reasons at all. The fact that many theists want theism to be true tells us nothing about the existence or quality of their reasons for thinking that theism is true.

It gets worse. To see why, let's do a thought experiment. Suppose you are arrested, put on trial, convicted for a crime you *did* commit, and are sentenced to prison. You probably wouldn't say to yourself, "Well, I don't want to live as if I am going to prison, so I'm going to invent a bunch of arguments in order to justify the belief that I am not going to prison." While it's possible that someone might do that,[31] probably virtually everyone would accept the reality that they are going to prison. To be sure, they might complain about things (such as the fairness of the law, the judge, or the sentence), but they wouldn't deny the reality that they were going to prison. By analogy, even if an atheist doesn't want to live as if God exists, it doesn't follow that the atheist would pretend to think that atheism is true while knowing "deep down" that God exists.

Besides, this interpretation of atheism just assumes that all atheists want to "live as if God does not exist" and *that* desire outweighs any other desires atheists might have. So far as I can tell, that assumption is false. First, though I don't have the data to back this up, I suspect that even most atheists wish that some sort of life after death is true. (They may not want to live forever and they may want a different kind of afterlife than the one offered by Christianity, but that's beside the point.) And any sane, rational person desires to avoid torture, especially *eternal* torture in hell. It's not obvious why anyone should think that those desires would *always* be outweighed by the desire to "live as if God does not exist."

Second, the Rebellion Thesis doesn't explain why a non-Christian's "rebellion" takes the form of (professed) atheism, as opposed to a myriad of other forms. If we are to believe that people have engaged in willful self-deception about God, there are many ways they could have false beliefs

---

31. It would be fascinating to find out if, in fact, anything like this has ever happened in human history.

about God. Most of those ways do not involve atheism. For example, someone could believe that their sinful behavior is permitted or even commanded by God. Or a person could believe that universalism is true in a way that there are no consequences for sinful behavior.

Third, the Rebellion Thesis doesn't explain the apparent conversions of people from atheism to theism. It seems much easier to explain both professions of atheism and professed converts from atheism to theism, on the assumption that at least *some* of those people are telling the truth than on the assumption that *all* of them are lying (or self-deceived).

RR: Jeff, you mentioned above that you wish theism were true. I suspect that will be a surprise to many people, and speaking on their behalf, I'd like to hear more about your position. I'm also wondering what you might say to a theist who would be inclined to dismiss your amiable testimony as a disingenuous attempt to conceal your real hostility against God. Yeah, I know, not very charitable, but some Christians are probably thinking it, so I have to ask.

JL: You're probably right that that will be a surprise to many people, but it shouldn't be. The fact that I have argued against God's existence should not lead someone to believe that I am indifferent to God's existence or even hopeful that God does not exist. If you'll pardon the analogy, I am very, very confident that I am not a millionaire, but no one should conclude from that belief that I don't wish I were a millionaire or even that I am indifferent about becoming one!

I wish theism were true for at least three reasons: (1) the opportunity to live longer than the short amount of time I'll get on earth; (2) the guarantee of perfect justice; and (3) the possibilities that would come from fellowship with God. Regarding (1), I don't know if I want *eternal* life or not, but I do know I'd like to live longer than a human lifetime, however long that turns out to be in my case. As for (2), while the demands of morality contribute to human flourishing more often than the average person recognizes, naturalism by definition posits an indifferent universe. Naturalism does not *guarantee* perfect justice. I wish it were the case, however, that everyone will ultimately be rewarded and punished based on what they deserve. Regarding (3), it seems to be true by definition that, if God exists, nothing could be more valuable to human beings than to have a relationship with God. But, by the same reason, that seems to be the strongest reason *possible* for wanting God to exist—at least, that seems to be the case if we assume that it is possible for beings like us to have a relationship with God.

As for the accusation that I am concealing my "real hostility against God," that accusation used to make me angry. My reaction is quite different now, however. I've come to recognize that *atheism is a risk* and so I mentally categorize the "atheists are hostile to God" response as just one of a spectrum of responses to what I call the "risk(s) of atheism." To be more precise, I've realized that *atheists coming out of the closet* and *atheists who defend arguments for atheism* are risks. How and why are they risks? I think this is best answered by paraphrasing something risk communication expert Peter Sandman said about gay rights, not atheism:

> For those who were comfortable before atheists who came out of the closet and defended arguments for atheism, atheists doing these things can seem (to theists) unfamiliar, beyond their control, and even morally threatening (for those theists who believe that morality somehow depends on God). Furthermore, probably most atheists are naturalists. Naturalism represents a worldview that probably most people *dread,* since it entails there is no afterlife. Encountering atheists, perhaps especially atheists who defend cases for atheism, may remind some theists of things they prefer to ignore (such as their own doubts about God's existence).[32]

What would I say to people who react to the risk of atheism with a denial of atheist sincerity? Well, I think the first thing I would say is that I understand the fear of doubt, the fear of personal mortality, and the fear of living in an indifferent universe. That is something I had to deal with as I gradually deconverted from Christian theism to atheism. I suspect the same is true of many, if not most or all, atheist deconverts.

In my case, it was my passionate desire to make sense of the world that led me to studying arguments for and against God's existence. While I do think the weight of the evidence favors naturalism over theism, I don't rule out the possibility of theistic evidence. In fact, in my own study of inductive logic, I've come to realize that the same logical principles which support the arguments for naturalism can also support the arguments for theism. And so I've publicly defended two lines of evidence for theism (consciousness and moral agency). I've also stated my intuition tells me there is some fact

---

32. Many atheists tend to assume that debates like these are always about "the data" (i.e., evidence for or against God's existence); I am grateful to Peter M. Sandman for helping me to understand that it is *not* all about the data. See Sandman, "Gay Rights as a Risk Communication Problem."

about morality which favors theism over naturalism (though showing this has turned out to be much harder than many theists think it is). The result is that I have caused some atheists to have the impression that I am a theist and many more atheists to complain that I am giving (undeserved) credibility to theistic arguments.

For my part, I think that if I have both some theists and some atheists questioning my motives, I must be doing something right.

RR: Jeff, thanks so much for sharing with us. You've been a generous and articulate interlocutor. I have appreciated your willingness to lay out your intellectual case for atheism with precision and verve. And as for the Rebellion Thesis, I share your concerns and I too believe that substantial evidence supports the existence of those "nonresistant nonbelievers" to which you refer. Finally, I can resonate with your experience of taking fire from both sides. I too have taken my share, and I'd also like to think that means I'm doing something right!

Some other atheists who aren't in rebellion

Well, there we go. As you can see, Jeff is a smart and thoughtful fellow. It is clear that he is able to articulate reasonable grounds to explain his unbelief which are far more sophisticated than the grounds for belief that would be offered by the vast majority of theists. For our purposes it is even more important to note that Jeff makes his case without any evident rancor or hostility. In short, Jeff doesn't seem to be angry at God. (For the record, he doesn't seem to be angry at the church either, at least insofar as I'm a representative of the church and he didn't get angry at me!) And as such, Jeff's testimony provides evidence against the Rebellion Thesis.

Before moving on, I'm going to say a bit more about the existence of irenic atheists like Jeff. Over the years I've known many atheists ranging from passing acquaintances to good friends. And while I've detected hostility in some, it is by no means universal. On the whole, I haven't found atheists to be any angrier or more hostile than anybody else. At the risk of belaboring the point, I will take a moment to recall a couple more examples.

First up, a couple years ago I was out to dinner with an atheist friend. (By the way, he picked up the tab because he's just that kind of guy. And since we're on the topic, I'll note that I haven't found Christians to be any more likely to pick up the tab than atheists.) During the conversation I mentioned that I experience God every day. My friend seemed particularly intrigued by that claim, not hostile, not incredulous, not dismissive, but rather intrigued. That impression was confirmed a day later when I received an email from him that asked pointedly: "You said that you experience God every day. Why don't *I* experience God?" With that question my friend had flagged the problem of divine hiddenness which Jeff mentioned in passing. And that's a huge question. To put it very briefly, if there is a God then why doesn't he make his presence more obvious to more people, especially those folk who genuinely want to know if he exists? People who appear to be nonresistant? People like my friend? That's a great question.

Okay, let's consider one more example and then we're moving on. A few years ago when I was at an academic conference I had a long conversation with a brilliant young philosopher who was completing his doctorate. He described how he had gradually lost his Christian faith after doing a close historical and philosophical examination of his beliefs. (By the way, during this time he was studying philosophy at a department that was predominantly Christian, so it is difficult to attribute his deconversion to the influence of anti-Christian tutelage.) I didn't agree with his conclusions, but I could sympathize with the process of reasoning that got him there. Indeed, I wish more Christians showed the careful, reflective acumen and commitment to seeking the truth demonstrated by this philosopher. Nor did I detect any anger or hostility in his deconversion story. In other words, here was yet another person directly contradicting the claims of the Rebellion Thesis.

Now it's time to close this chapter and move on. Thus far I have considered both biblical and empirical evidence for the Rebellion Thesis. On both accounts I think the evidence is unequivocal that the thesis ought to be rejected. But before putting it to rest for good, we need to consider certain high profile cases where atheists make statements that seem to corroborate the Rebellion Thesis. And we shall devote the next chapter to addressing them.

5

What about the atheists who say they don't want there to be a God?

The 2012 presidential election between Barack Obama and Mitt Romney was a fiercely fought campaign. While it had many pivotal moments, arguably the most significant occurred on May 17th, although nobody knew it at the time. On that day Romney was speaking at a private fundraiser during which he was secretly recorded making a comment about a sizeable portion of the American population. This is what he said: "There are 47 percent of the people who will vote for the president no matter what . . . who are dependent upon government, who believe that they are victims. . . . These are people who pay no income tax . . . and so my job is not to worry about those people. I'll never convince them that they should take personal responsibility and care for their lives."[1] Four months later in September, the magazine *Mother Jones* released the 47 percent video, and its inflammatory content helped put Romney on the defensive for the rest of the campaign. Indeed, as 2012 drew to a close, Romney's 47 percent comment was chosen by Yale Law School as the most notable quotation of the year.[2]

For our purposes, the interesting thing about the Romney gaffe was the way that it played into common progressive assumptions about the true beliefs and motivations of Republicans. For many progressives, Romney wasn't merely sharing his own view. Rather, he was providing a revelation of the true spirit of conservatism. As Stephanie Brooks observes,

1. Cited in Margolin, "Romney's 47% Comment Named Quote of the Year."
2. Ibid.

> Here was a glimpse of the real views that lie beneath the carefully
> polished exterior of the micromanaged politician. This plays into a
> well-established campaign narrative that says if we can simply de-
> code the spin—or even better, catch the candidate off guard—we
> will discover what they *really* think. In this conception there is an
> authentic political self, hidden from voters behind all the bells and
> whistles of the campaign.[3]

As a result, a revealing moment like the 47 percent comment can be
seen to provide insight not only into the Romney campaign, but also into
conservatism itself. In short, it seems to justify the well-established narrative of the cold conservative who is pro-rich and cares little for the poor
and disenfranchised. Whether such grand extrapolations are warranted is
another question, of course, but the fact is that people do make them.

It seems to me that we can find similar reasoning when it comes to
Christian perspectives of atheists. As a result, we can critique the biblical
exegesis that is invoked as scriptural support for the Rebellion Thesis. And
we can provide empirical evidence of non-hostile atheists to show the thesis
also doesn't match up with lived reality. But even so, we are not quite done
until we address the role that high profile and allegedly revelatory atheist quotes play in propping up the Rebellion Thesis. The fact is that many
Christian apologists appeal to particular quotes from atheists, quotes that
are presented as revealing something of the true spirit of atheism. In the
same way that Romney's 47 percent quip was taken by many progressives to
reveal something about conservatism generally, so many Christian apologists take select atheist quotes to reveal something about atheism generally.

Let me state at the outset that I consider this an illegitimate way to
seek to support the Rebellion Thesis. Indeed, in my opinion this attempt
to prop up the Rebellion Thesis by appealing to a select set of quotations
amounts to little more than a baldly subjective attempt to confirm one's
own prejudices. Let me put it this way: who decides which quotes represent
the true spirit of atheism? For example, why not take Jeff's amiable presentation of atheism in chapter 4 as providing a revealing insight into atheism?
Why not take the testimony of other putative nonresistant nonbelievers?
The answer seems to be that prior assumptions sourced in the Rebellion
Thesis predetermine which quotes will be seen as especially insightful. And
that leads me to conclude that this method is crippled by an unchecked
confirmation bias (that psychological disposition to select evidence that

---

3. Brooks, "The Art of the Campaign Gaffe."

supports our views whilst ignoring evidence that contradicts them). Bottom line: you can't justify sweeping statements about Republicans based on one Romney quote, and you can't justify sweeping statements about atheists based on one (or a few) select atheist quotes.

Now that I've logged my concerns I can turn to consider the many others who seem to consider this a valid way to justify popular opinions about atheism. With this point in mind, we are going to dedicate this chapter to taking a closer look at the way that Christians appeal to select atheist quotes as justification for the Rebellion Thesis, and we will do so with special attention to the oft-cited words of two atheists, Christopher Hitchens and Thomas Nagel.

Can you really be angry at a God that you don't believe in?

Before we consider these select rebellion quotes, I want to address an objection to the very possibility that an atheist could be in rebellion against God. The point was raised by Jeff during our conversation in chapter 4. As he observed, "it's hard to hate someone (or Someone) you think doesn't exist. I, for one, have no idea how that is supposed to work: how would anyone generate emotional outrage towards a *non-existent* person?" Other atheists have made the same point. In their book *50 Great Myths about Atheism* Russell Blackford and Udo Schüklenk set about to debunk the myth that "Atheists Hate or are Angry with God." And they begin like this: "Let us start with a pretty obvious point: atheists cannot be angry with God, and we cannot resent God . . . because we do not believe God actually exists. How could you hate or resent something you do not think exists?"[4]

I may not agree with the claim that *all* atheists are in rebellion against (or angry at) God. But can we justify the alternative extreme suggested here, namely that *none* are? Before offering a response to this atheist rejoinder, it is worth pointing out that there is a definite advantage for atheists to argue that no atheist could be hostile toward God. The advantage arises from the fact that when a person has a high emotional investment in a topic they are less likely to be objective about it. Thus, if you can show you don't have that high emotional investment or personal stake in a particular topic (e.g., "I don't have a horse in that race!"), you provide a *prima face* reason to trust your objectivity about that topic.

---

4. Blackford and Schüklenk, *50 Great Myths About Atheism*, 21.

Consider the following illustration. Jones is Smith's workplace supervisor. If Smith discovers that his boss (Jones) personally loathes him, Smith will have reason to question the objectivity of the performance reports about him that Jones submits to management. To put it bluntly, if Jones hates Smith, then we have a reason to question whether Jones can provide an honest and reliable appraisal of Smith's abilities.

With that in mind, if it turns out that atheists could not possibly be negatively disposed toward God, then that would count in favor of the general objectivity of atheists, at least to the extent that it would ensure that atheist reasoning is not clouded by a distorting hostility toward God. To be sure, this would still not guarantee that atheists will be perfectly rational in their reasoning about God. But it would at least secure the conclusion that their reasoning will never be distorted by any degree of hostility toward God.

While I agree that the objection raised by Jeff Lowder, Blackford, and Schüklenk is reasonable at first blush, I also believe that further reflection supports the conclusion that there are indeed ways that an atheist could be negatively disposed toward God. Those ways just need to be appropriately qualified. At this point I'm going to consider two ways.

To begin with, an atheist could be hostile toward God in virtue of *hoping* God doesn't exist. The first thing to recognize here is that *believing* and *hoping* are different things and they are not tethered together. Thus, what I believe could be quite different from what I hope. For example, I might believe I'm going to lose my job, but I hope I don't. Or (to refer back to Jeff's example), I might believe I won't win the lottery, but I hope I do.

When it comes to atheism, some atheists may believe there is no God, but they hope there is. Indeed, this was the position that Jeff Lowder took in our conversation. While some atheists are like Jeff in hoping that God does exist, others are insistent in their hope that God doesn't exist. In other words, if some atheists evince nonresistant nonbelief, others appear disposed to *resistant* nonbelief. And it would appear that both Christopher Hitchens and Thomas Nagel can be counted in that latter group. This leads me to the final point: when atheists hope God doesn't exist, that hope can be reasonably taken, at least in some cases, to indicate at least some degree of hostility toward God. Put more precisely, it would be hostility directed at the *concept* or *idea* of God, a hostility that would be transferred to God himself should the atheist come to believe he does exist.

This brings us to the second (and related) way to think about this hostility. In addition to hoping God doesn't exist, an atheist might also be prepared to oppose God should it happen that he does exist. We can illustrate the point with the following analogy. A man returns to his hometown in Kansas only to discover that it has just been almost completely destroyed. For several blocks, houses are reduced to rubble, power lines are down, and people are lying dead and injured in the streets. The man's first thought is that the town was destroyed by a powerful tornado. In other words, the man doesn't believe any human being is responsible for the carnage he is witnessing. At the same time, the man also concludes that *if* there was some human being(s) behind the destruction of his town (e.g., an assault by Al Qaeda) then he would hate the perpetrator(s) of this violence and he would rebel against them. But until he knows otherwise, he will continue to attribute the destruction to a wayward tornado.

Think of that destroyed town as analogous to the world around us, a world often beset with great carnage and immense suffering. The atheist looks out and attributes the sorry state of the world to wholly natural causes (like the tornado). But if the atheist came to believe there was a God responsible for the lamentable state of the world, he would rebel against the deity as surely as the bereaved resident would rebel against any terrorist aggressors of the town. This predisposition to rebel is certainly indicative of hostility, at least *in potentia*.

Real life instances of this kind of hostility toward God are not hard to come by. Some years ago I witnessed a debate on the existence of God between atheist Henry Morgentaler and Christian apologist William Lane Craig. During the question period after the formal debate, a young man posed the following question to Morgentaler: "If it could be proven to you that God exists, would you bow to him?" Morgentaler could hardly conceal his disdain for the question and snapped back that he would bow to no one.[5]

At first blush, Morgentaler's response might seem inconceivable to a Christian. How could it possibly make sense to refuse to bow to the creator and sustainer of the universe? However, it might help to keep in mind that Morgentaler was a Jew who survived the Nazi concentration camps. In light of the suffering and evil that Morgentaler witnessed, it is not a stretch to imagine that his hostility toward God parallels the hostility of the grieving

5. I discuss this case under the rubric of "protest atheism" in *Finding God in the Shack*, 117.

Kansan toward anybody who would inflict such egregious destruction on his town.

In conclusion, conceptually we can see how it is perfectly reasonable that an atheist could be hostile toward God in the sense that she hopes God doesn't exist and that she is prepared to oppose God should it happen that he does exist. What is more, real life cases like that of Henry Morgentaler provide additional empirical support for the claim.

We also shouldn't miss the implication that if it is possible for atheists to be hostile toward God, it follows that this hostility could potentially distort their reasoning about God in the same way that a theist's affinity for God could do so. For example, just as the theist may exercise a confirmation bias in favor of evidence *for* God's existence so the hostile atheist could exercise a bias in favor of evidence *against* God's existence. This supports the general conclusion that both theists and atheists are emotionally invested as they reason about God's existence and nature.

It also follows from this that while the Rebellion Thesis is lacking in biblical and empirical evidence, it isn't incoherent. And with that in mind, we can now turn to those high profile quotes that some Christians appeal to as support for the thesis. Could these quotes provide the evidence the thesis so desperately needs?

Atheists who don't want there to be a God

In our discussion in chapter 4, Jeff observed that the best evidence for the Rebellion Thesis will likely be found in "quotations from atheists (such as Thomas Nagel) who appear to hope that theism is false." I think Jeff is right about this. While I may not view the prospects of this avenue to be very bright, it does remain the best hope for the faltering Rebellion Thesis. One can find many Christians appealing to such paradigm instances of hostility toward God as evidence that atheism generally is constituted by rebellion against God. Their reasoning is given some credibility by the fact that there are some atheists who appear to fit the profile described by the Rebellion Thesis. Included in their ranks we find the recently deceased new atheist Christopher Hitchens (d. 2011) and the world renowned philosopher Thomas Nagel. In this section we will examine some key comments from Hitchens and Nagel which could be taken to indicate their hostility toward God and rebellion against him. As we proceed we should keep the following two questions in mind. First, do we know that the statement in question is really indicative of rebellion against God? Second, assuming that this statement is indicative of rebellion against God, can it justify the conclusion that *all* instances of atheism are likewise instances of rebellion against God?

We will begin with Christopher Hitchens, new atheist, author of the bestselling book *God is Not Great,* and popularizer of the moniker "*anti-theist,*" a term that he himself embraced with aplomb. In *God is Not Great* Hitchens explains that antitheism is "the view that we ought to be glad that none of the religious myths has any truth to it, or in it."[6] While Hitchens's immediate target in this quote is "religion," the existence of God is central to many of these "religious myths" that Hitchens rejects. Thus, it is clear that God is Hitchens's proximate target, and in virtue of hoping that all religions are false he also hopes that God doesn't exist.

Whenever I encounter a rejection of "religion" as sweeping and un-qualified as that which Hitchens gives us, I can't help but wonder whether (or to what degree) that rejection might be fueled by a misunderstanding of some of those "myths." Could it be that Hitchens is not really rejecting religion (or God)? Could it be that his rejection instead is directed at some particularly crude expressions of religious/theistic belief? We've already considered the extent to which the bad behavior of Christians or other religious people might unwittingly fuel religiously hostile sentiments. The same may be said for errant beliefs about God. I'm thinking here about the old line, "tell me about the God you don't believe in, because I probably don't believe in him either." So *what kind of God* does Hitchens not believe in? Can he be more specific?

In *God is Not Great* Hitchens focuses his critiques on the biblical por-traits of God. But in his essay "The Gospel according to Mel," he stresses that his opposition extends also to the most sophisticated constructions of the theologians and philosophers. Hitchens makes the point by focusing in particular on the famous philosophical theologian Paul Tillich who devel-oped a more abstract and sophisticated theology, precisely with the hope of wooing skeptics. Alas, Hitchens wasn't impressed by Tillich or his epigones:

> I discover when I read the claims of even the more meek Tillich-like theologians that I am relieved that they are untrue. I would positively detest the all-embracing, refulgent, stress-free embrace that they propose. I have no wish to live in some Disneyland of the mind and spirit, some Nirvana of utter null completeness. Religion's promise to deliver this is in my opinion plainly false.

6. Hitchens, *God is Not Great,* 102.

But what it can deliver me is the prospect of serfdom, mental and physical, and the chance to live under fantastic and cruel laws, or to be subjected to frantic violence.[7]

With this passage Hitchens appears to slam the door shut to theism of any sort. His hostility is not directed merely at some particularly crude brand of religion. He really doesn't believe in God, and he doesn't want God to exist. His objection is not directed merely to one or another inadequate or unsophisticated portrait of God. His quarrel is not merely with the God of a populist fundamentalism or, for that matter, a woolly progressivism. Rather, he objects to the very idea of God, even when it is dressed up with all the intellectual sophistication that an erudite theologian like Paul Tillich can muster. He repudiates wholesale the notion of a divine mind that created and sustains the universe and directs it to his own ends.

And why is Hitchens in such forceful opposition to the existence of a divine being? Because, as he seems to think, God's existence is a noxious idea that would reduce the noble human being to the role of a mere serf on the land of a powerful divine overlord. In other words, if we embrace God then we abdicate true human freedom and autonomy. And that's not a trade that Hitchens is willing to make.

Our second example is found in a much discussed passage from Thomas Nagel's 1997 book *The Last Word*. Nagel's testimony is particularly relevant here because while Hitchens was an iconoclastic rhetorician with an ax to grind, Nagel is a deeply respected and sober philosopher, a professor at New York University and the author of such critically acclaimed books as *The View from Nowhere* and *Mortal Questions*. What is more, while Hitchens is unabashedly partisan in his critiques of religion, Nagel is measured and very fair. One can find evidence of Nagel's objectivity in the fact that he has occasionally angered many in the broader atheist community, and endured substantial derision as a result, by endorsing positions or making arguments at odds with majority atheist opinion.[8]

7. Hitchens, "The Gospel according to Mel," 338.

8. In his book *Mind and Cosmos*, Nagel argues that the reigning philosophical paradigm among contemporary atheists—a position called naturalism—is a failure and should be replaced with another philosophical theory. This thesis rankled many atheists who believed the attack on naturalism was unjustified. Equally controversial was Nagel's high profile endorsement in the *Times Literary Supplement* of Christian intelligent design theorist Stephen Meyer's monograph *Signature in the Cell* as one of the best books of 2009. Whether you agree with him or not, Nagel speaks the truth as he sees it without lens-distorting party-line commitments.

With that in mind, Nagel's candid observations about atheism in *The Last Word* have attracted a lot of attention from theists. He wrote:

> I *want* atheism to be true and am made uneasy by the fact that some of the most intelligent and well-informed people I know are religious believers. It isn't just that I don't believe in God and, naturally, hope that I'm right in my belief. It's that *I hope there is no God! I don't want there to be a God; I don't want the universe to be like that.*
>
> My guess is that *this cosmic authority problem is not a rare condition* and that it is responsible for much of the scientism and reductionism of our time.[9]

It's not surprising that this quote should have caught the attention of Christians committed to the Rebellion Thesis. After all, as already noted, Nagel is a leading philosopher and an independent thinker so his testimony immediately carries far more weight than your typical new atheist polemicist. Moreover, after beginning with a reflection on his own state of unbelief, he then opines that many atheists share the same "cosmic authority problem." Now that's starting to sound promising. In the accompanying footnote, Nagel refuses to speculate on which sources, Oedipal or otherwise, might explain the genesis of this aversion. This in turn leaves it open for the Christian to attribute that opposition to sin, just as the Rebellion Thesis supposes.

Given the "47 percent" aura of this quote, it shouldn't surprise us that several Christians have appealed to it as support for the Rebellion Thesis. Steven Cowan and James S. Spiegel draw attention to the passage in their book *The Love of Wisdom*: "Nagel, like others, has a problem with 'cosmic authority.' He doesn't want there to be an omnipotent, omniscient, and wholly good deity to hold him accountable."[10] Even more significant, in his commentary on the quote, Douglas Groothuis opines that Nagel's words harken back to Paul's description of cosmic rebellion: "Nagel's visceral disclosure resembles the apostle Paul's description of those who, in opposition to the divine knowledge of which they have access, suppress the truth of God's existence, fail to give God thanks, and thus become darkened in their understanding (see Rom 1:18–21)."[11]

---

9. Nagel, *The Last Word*, 130, emphasis added.

10. Cowan and Spiegel, *The Love of Wisdom*, 256.

11. Groothuis, "Why Truth Matters Most," 444. See also Moreland and Issler, *In Search of a Confident Faith*, 59. Other Christian apologists are more nuanced in their

Perhaps Cowan, Spiegel, and Groothuis are on to something. It is true that the Rebellion Thesis doesn't look quite as outrageous after considering Nagel's quote. Add to this the self-described antitheist Hitchens as he gripes about "the prospect of serfdom" under God and you just might see a pattern emerging. So could it be that Nagel is demonstrating that this cosmic authority problem really does bring us to the heart of atheism? To put it another way, did Nagel inadvertently produce his own "47 percent" quote, one which lays bare the intransigent spirit of atheism?

As we consider whether Nagel's quote supports the Rebellion Thesis, let's start by noting that Nagel himself nowhere suggests that *all* atheism can be attributed to a "cosmic authority problem." He merely speculates that many instances could be. He also suggests that there is nobody neutral about the existence of God.[12] But one simply can't support the Rebellion Thesis based on those comparatively meager results.

What is more, a careful reading of *The Last Word* suggests that Nagel provides at least one explanation for this aversion toward God which is not, in fact, driven by antitheistic hostility. In the following passage Nagel offers a fascinating speculation on the ultimate source of this aversion, and this source is not tied to any problem with cosmic authority *per se*:

> there is really no reason to assume that the only alternative to an evolutionary explanation of everything is a religious one. However, this may not be comforting enough, because the feeling that I have called the fear of religion *may extend far beyond the existence of a personal god, to include any cosmic order of which mind is an irreducible and nonaccidental part.* I suspect that there is *a deepseated aversion in the modern "disenchanted" Weltanschauung to any ultimate principles that are not dead*—that is, devoid of any reference to the possibility of life or consciousness.[13]

Note that in this passage Nagel suggests that the aversion to God may in fact be sourced in a more fundamental aversion to, or even fear of, ultimate explanatory principles that are personal in nature. If Nagel is right about this then his problem, and that of other atheists like him, may not be that they are against God, but rather that they have an aversion to unknowable or mysterious personal explanations.

---

appeal to Nagel's quote. See, for example, Copan, *That's Just Your Interpretation*, 21.

12. Nagel, *The Last Word*, 130, n.

13. Ibid., 133, emphasis added.

Perhaps you're not exactly clear about what Nagel is referring to here, so let me try an illustration to unpack his speculation a bit further. Imagine that there is an indigenous tribe living beside some sweeping sand dunes. Day after day there is a low, mysterious hum emitting from the sand dunes and the indigenous people attribute that hum to a supernatural cause, i.e., mysterious spirits that live in the dunes. Many Western visitors to this community would not only be inclined to think there is a natural explanation, but they also might *prefer* there to be a natural explanation. Why? This could be for at least two reasons. To begin with, the Westerners would prefer the parsimony (that is, the simplicity) and familiarity of a picture of the world in which novel phenomena can ultimately be attributable to natural causes. In addition, those Westerners might simply find the notion of spiritual agencies wandering the dunes to be unsettling.

And why exactly is this unsettling? Well, consider another illustration closer to home. Indeed, it could be *in* your home. When I hear a strange bump in the night, I *could* attribute it to a ghost, but I'd certainly prefer to think it was the dog! The prospect of unknown (and perhaps unknowable) nonphysical personal agencies interacting in our world is indeed unsettling. It isn't that the Westerners are necessarily *hostile* to spirit beings humming in the dunes. But they hope such beings don't exist just the same. In a very interesting passage in *The Problem of Pain* C. S. Lewis locates this fear, this aversion, with respect to Rudolf Otto's conception of the *numinous*:

> Suppose you were told there was a tiger in the next room: you would know that you were in danger and would probably feel fear. But if you were told "There is a ghost in the next room," and believed it, you would feel, indeed, what is often called fear, but of a different kind. It would not be based on the knowledge of danger, for no one is primarily afraid of what a ghost may do to him, but of the mere fact that it is a ghost. It is "uncanny" rather than dangerous, and the special kind of fear it excites may be called Dread. With the Uncanny one has reached the fringes of the Numinous. Now suppose that you were told simply "There is a mighty spirit in the room," and believed it. Your feelings would then be even less like the mere fear of danger: but the disturbance would be profound. You would feel wonder and a certain shrinking—a sense of inadequacy to cope with such a visitant and of prostration before it—an emotion which might be expressed in Shakespeare's words "Under it my genius is rebuked." This feeling may be described as awe, and the object which excites it as the *Numinous*.[14]

14. Lewis, *The Problem of Pain*, 17.

As Lewis points out, the fear of the ghost is quite different from the fear of the tiger. It is a fear that appears to overlap significantly with Nagel's aversion to *"ultimate principles that are not dead."* The key to recognize is that this aversion (which, in its purest form, Otto referred to as the *mysterium tremendum*) is not necessarily indicative of hatred or hostility. Instead, it is closer to that uncanny fear of the unknown, like Lewis's ghost in the next room, or mysterious entities wandering the sand dunes.[15]

Speaking of those entities in the sand dunes, let's return to that illustration for a moment. The indigenous people in the illustration represent a perspective that we can call the "enchanters" while the Westerners represent the "disenchanters" position. Enchanters tend to be drawn to magic and mystery and mental agencies. Consequently, they seem to find ultimate personal explanations and the numinous to be appealing. By contrast, the disenchanters prefer natural and scientific explanations that appeal to matter, energy, and forces. In their sociological study of atheism in America, sociologists Williamson and Yancey effectively contrast the two perspectives:

> For many believers [i.e., enchanters], this may seem a dismal thought—that there is no mystery, that there is no "other," and that there is no eternal father to protect and comfort them. For many nonbelievers [i.e., disenchanters], though, the idea is liberating: no fear of death and no fear of judgment, just a marvelous universe to experience and explore—empirically.[16]

To be sure, the disenchanter's perspective is consistent with some degree of active rebellion against God. The desire to avoid divine judgment, for example, could reinforce a predisposition to the disenchanter's position. But the key for us is that we simply don't know to what extent Nagel's aversion toward God is generated by antitheistic impulses versus a more general aversion to the Uncanny side of life. It could be that Nagel maintains a preference for a simpler, predictable, and familiar world that is reducible to certain fundamental material principles. And thus it is for that reason

---

15. In 1974 Canadian singer Burton Cummings walked into St. Thomas Church in New York and was suddenly overcome with the sense of a presence he could not understand, a presence very much like Lewis's Uncanny and Otto's *mysterium tremendum*. After this unsettling experience Cummings wrote a song about it that became a big hit. He called the song "I'm Scared."

16. Williamson and Yancey, *There is No God*, 12.

that he hopes atheism is true. Consequently, we simply don't have enough information to count Nagel's comment as evidence for the Rebellion Thesis.

Nagel gives us a bit more on what I'm calling the disenchanter position elsewhere in *The Last Word* when he ties this drive for disenchantment to the laudable desire to have explanations that we can understand. As he puts it, "the idea of God serves as a placeholder for an explanation where something seems to demand explanation and none is available . . . ."[17] Further, he adds, "I have never been able to understand the idea of God well enough to see such a theory as truly explanatory: It seems rather to stand for a still unspecified purposiveness that itself remains unexplained."[18] From this perspective Nagel's aversion to God is an aversion to giving up the quest for further understanding. Once again, we see that we need not attribute his words to any divine rebellion.

When we draw all these points together we find that Nagel's initial comment offers very little to support a robust Rebellion Thesis. It is true that Nagel speculates that many atheists may have a cosmic authority problem, but he never suggests that *all* do. Moreover, he also offers another plausible explanation for the desire that God not exist, one that is rooted not in an aversion to divine authority, but rather in the disenchanter's drive for simplicity, predictability, and explanations that can be grasped by the human mind. And as Lewis illustrates, every one of us can sympathize with this impulse, at least to some degree. (I sure *hope* that thump in the next room wasn't caused by a ghost.) To cap it off, Nagel also warns atheists about allowing preferences to color their reasoning. At one point he cautions, "it is just as irrational to be influenced in one's beliefs by the hope that God does not exist as by the hope that God does exist."[19]

To sum up, while Nagel's quote allows for the possibility that an indeterminate number of atheists may be in rebellion against God, it simply does not provide good evidence for the Rebellion Thesis. If I may be blunt, it seems to me that Christians who attempt to play isolated quotes like that of Nagel as a "47 percent trump card" to support of the Rebellion Thesis are engaged in little more than quote-mining. (And yes, quote-mining *is* as bad as it sounds.)

17. Nagel, *The Last Word*, 132–33.
18. Ibid., 75–76.
19. Ibid., 131.

Is it irrational to oppose God?

I argued above that the notion of atheists being hostile to God is perfectly coherent so long as we understand that to mean the atheist hopes God doesn't exist and/or is prepared to oppose God if he does exist. However, from another angle it would appear that this kind of opposition to God is *not* coherent. To see why, we need to begin with a minimal definition of what we mean when we say "God." I already provided a definition in chapter 4 which is couched in the terms of classical theism. According to this understanding, "God is a necessary agent who is omnipotent, omniscient, omnipresent, and perfectly good (or omnibenevolent)." This definition can be distilled further to the descriptor famously proposed by Anselm, according to which God is *that being than which none greater can be conceived.*

Let's proceed with the Anselmian definition in mind as we turn to consider this incoherence that I've suggested resides in the antitheistic position. Here's the key point: while a person might believe God (defined in Anselmian terms) does not exist, given the definition of the deity as maximally great, a person ought to *hope* God exists. And that means that it is incoherent to be opposed to the existence of this maximally great being.

While this point seems obvious to me, it apparently doesn't seem so to others like Hitchens and Nagel (who are both presumably familiar with the Anselmian definition). Given that fact, I'm going to spend some time unpacking the logic. And I'm going to begin with an illustration. Consider the case of Ollie, a ten-year-old boy living in an orphanage in Victorian London. Ollie was found as a toddler wandering the muddy streets of the city, crying and holding a worn blue blanket. For the last eight years Ollie has lived in the orphanage and it has been, by any stretch of the imagination, a hard life. He sleeps on a filthy straw mattress where bed bugs and mice are his nocturnal companions. In the daytime he suffers beatings from the larger boys and the headmaster. Every day of the year his meals are the same: a pasty, tasteless gruel which is made (or so the older boys say) from the slop that pigs refuse to eat. His only joy is a bag of candy that he receives from a group of nuns every December.

Late one night Ollie is sitting on his straw mattress in the chilly room listening to the rats scurrying and the horses and carriages rolling by on the streets below when Johnny calls out to him in the darkness.

> "Pssst, hey Ollie!"
> "What is it Johnny?" Ollie replies.

"Wouldn't it be great to have a wonderful dad out there some-where? A *wonderdad!* He's the best dad in the world, better than you could ever imagine. And he loves you very much. For some reason that you can't understand you were separated from him when you were a baby. But he's going to come for you one day and make everything right. Wouldn't that be amazing?" Johnny says dreamily.

One might expect Ollie to respond with an enthusiastic, "Yes, I hope there is a wonderdad out there for me!" But let's say that instead he replied, "No, I don't want there to be a wonderdad. I'd rather remain an orphan!" What could possibly explain such a response?

As I see it, there are a couple reasons that Ollie might respond in that fashion. To begin with, it could be that Ollie didn't take the question seriously. For example, it may be that when Johnny says "wonderdad," Ollie envisions some kind of deadbeat who really didn't have a good excuse for leaving him in the orphanage all those years. From that perspective it is no surprise that Ollie would decline the offer since he never seriously considered the possibility of having a wonderful father in the first place.

I suspect that first possibility describes the opposition of folks like Hitchens. After all, Hitchens claims to be rejecting the same God that Christians would embrace, that being than which none greater can be conceived. But then he describes life with God as equivalent to a form of mental and physical serfdom in which we endure "cruel laws" and are "subjected to frantic violence." However, if God really is the being than which none greater can be conceived then life in restored relationship with him wouldn't be cruel and violent; rather, it would be indescribably wonderful. Given this fact, it seems reasonable to conclude that Hitchens has not taken the question seriously to begin with.

To be sure, I can see *why* Hitchens might fall into this kind of misunderstanding. After all, religious documents like the Bible (and Qur'an) occasionally (frequently?) portray God as acting in ways that appear contrary to the Anselmian definition.[20] But in that case the reasonable response would not be to hope God does not exist (still less to oppose him if he does). Rather, the proper response would be to doubt that these prima facie contradictory claims are likely to be true should it happen that God does exist. One can also *hope* that these various claims are not true, should it happen that God does exist. But what one cannot coherently do is hope

20. Hitchens discusses some of that material in *God is Not Great*, chapters 7–10.

that God (aka that being than which none greater can be conceived) does not exist.

This brings me to the second possibility. Could it be that Ollie *did* understand Johnny's question and even so he still prefers to remain an orphan? That is possible, and from an emotional perspective it is even understandable. Just think about it. After years in the home, Ollie could have so much anger and bitterness built up that he might indeed choose his own current misery over a beautiful future of reconciliation with his wonderful father. But even if this is an emotionally understandable choice, that doesn't make it a rational one. Imagine that there is a wonderdad and one day he shows up at the orphanage ready to take Ollie home. Would the boy really turn his back on his father's smiling countenance and march back up the stairs to his cold room and straw mattress? If he did, I could only consider that embittered response a deeply irrational choice for self-imposed misery.

When it comes to atheists who express hostility toward God of the kinds noted above, I am left with these same two explanations. It could be that they are not really grasping what is on offer, a situation that once again calls to mind the quip "tell me about the God you don't believe in, because I probably don't believe in him either." Or it could be that they really do grasp the question and have instead resolved to make the irrational choice for bitterness and alienation. Again, while I might emotionally sympathize with the latter response, it still strikes me as a fundamentally irrational choice.

Is there rational rebellion against God?

There is probably no literary depiction of the atheist rebel more memorable than that of Ivan in Fyodor Dostoyevsky's great nineteenth-century novel *The Brothers Karamazov*. The heart of the book is found in the powerful debates on God, evil, and the meaning of life that unfold between Ivan and his pious brother Aloysha. The centerpiece of Ivan's outraged rejection of theism comes in the horrendous evils that are readily on display in the world around us. In Ivan's view the evil we find in the world strongly counts against God's goodness. What is more, it also counts against our willingness to hope that there might be a God to redeem this great big mess. At one point Ivan drives his view home by relaying the moving story of a young boy who was torn apart by hunting dogs at the direction of their rich master, all while his helpless mother watched in impotent agony.

Theologians are certainly aware of the problems Ivan raises and they have long sought to reconcile such awful evils with an omnipotent and perfectly good God. Perhaps the most common response has been the claim that God allows those evils because he has some greater good in view. But Ivan is not persuaded by that explanation. Indeed, "not persuaded" hardly conveys his indignation, for Ivan finds such claims outrageous and morally offensive. He cannot countenance the possibility of a God who planned the evils in the world with the intention of making it all okay, eventually. This is what he says in response:

> I don't want harmony. I don't want it, out of the love I bear to mankind. I want to remain with my suffering unavenged. I'd rather remain with my suffering unavenged and my indignation unappeased, *even if I were wrong*. Besides, too high a price has been placed on harmony. We cannot afford to pay so much for admission. And therefore I hasten to return my ticket of admission. And indeed, if I am an honest man, I'm bound to hand it back as soon as possible. This I am doing. It is not God that I do not accept, Alyosha. I merely most respectfully return him the ticket.[21]

Ivan clearly doesn't like the proposal that God plans the evil in the world with a good end in mind. But what is his problem, exactly? Just what is he saying here?

Let's start with the offense that everyone recognizes, namely the brutal murder of the child. Atheist and theist alike are aghast at this heinous crime. However, the greater goods theodicist seeks to make sense of it by claiming that God *foreknew* this murder would occur and so he *allowed* it to occur in order to achieve some "greater good." When the atheist is presented with that claim he hears not a satisfactory account of the murder, but rather *a crime that is added to the murder*. The very idea of allowing a child to be torn apart by wild dogs for a greater good is repulsive to Ivan. By Ivan's lights, the suggestion that God providentially allowed this unthinkable crime for a greater good doesn't redeem the crime; if anything, it *worsens* the problem by making God accessory to a heinous murder. And so, Ivan responds in the only way that seems morally appropriate: He insists that he doesn't *want* the harmony that comes with a murder planned for divine purposes. He'd prefer to be "left with the unavenged suffering."

When I look at the issue from Ivan's perspective, namely that of one atrocity (God's inaction) being invoked as a means to redeem another (the

---

21. Dostoyevsky, *The Brothers Karamazov*, 287.

boy's murder), I can understand where he is coming from. To be sure, I don't agree with Ivan's assessment any more than I agree with Ollie's. But at the same time, I am sympathetic with his reasoning. I can see how Ivan would view God's nonintervention in the face of great evil as turning him into the guilty bystander, as if God is the greatest violator of a Good Samaritan statute.

I also know that it is one thing to reflect on God and the problem of evil *in abstracto* and it is something else entirely to do so in the midst of great suffering. While the experience of suffering has driven many theists closer to God, it has also left others disillusioned and anguished. In his Nobel Prize winning memoir *Night*, a harrowing tale of life in the concentration camp, Elie Wiesel recalls one elderly Jewish rabbi who struggled with his faith:

> I knew a rabbi, from a small town in Poland. He was old and bent, his lips constantly trembling. He was always praying, in the block, at work, in the ranks. He recited entire pages from the Talmud, arguing with himself, asking and answering himself endless questions. One day, he said to me:
>
> "It's over. God is no longer with us."
>
> And as though he regretted having uttered such words so coldly, so dryly, he added in his broken voice, "I know. No one has the right to say things like that. I know that very well. Man is too insignificant, too limited, to even try to comprehend God's mysterious ways. But what can someone like myself do? I'm neither a sage nor a just man. I am not a saint. I'm a simple creature of flesh and bone. I suffer hell in my soul and my flesh. I also have eyes and I see what is being done here. Where is God's mercy? Where's God? How can I believe, how can anyone believe in this God of Mercy?"[22]

These are profound words and borne of the suffering from which they came they speak with a unique power and authority. Suffice it to say, atheists are not the only ones to ask how, in this world of suffering, we can possibly believe in a God of mercy. The religiously pious ask it as well. Indeed, how could a faith *not* be shaken when you contemplate the notion that every person gassed in the ovens and reduced to the ashes and vapor of the puffing smokestacks of Auschwitz was for a greater good? Ivan's response is

22. Wiesel, *Night*, 76–77.

to turn in his ticket. The rabbi's response is to fumble in anguish with his. Perhaps the faithful and the faithless are not as far apart as we had thought.[23]

We will draw this chapter to a close by returning to the case of Bob Jyono, which we first referenced in chapter 4. I first learned about the story of Mr. Jyono and his family from the infuriating and heartbreaking 2006 documentary *Deliver Us from Evil*.[24] Back in the 1970s the Jyonos were faithful Catholics living in California. Their priest, Oliver O'Grady, was very close to the family and over the years he stayed overnight at their house on multiple occasions. Twenty years later Bob and his wife were shocked to learn that O'Grady had been accused of raping several children in the diocese. Initially incredulous at the charges, they phoned their daughter Ann to tell her the news. However, Ann didn't respond with the shock they had expected. Instead, she quickly changed the subject and then said she had to go. In a horrifying moment of revelation, the Jyonos realized their daughter had been one of O'Grady's victims. Soon after, they discovered that O'Grady had repeatedly raped Ann over a period of *seven years,* and moreover that he had done so in their house and often while just steps from their bedroom.

As a parent I can't imagine coming to terms with the unthinkably horrifying revelation that the guest I had invited into my house on multiple occasions—and a man of the cloth no less!—had exploited that hospitality as an opportunity to victimize my child in the most heinous way imaginable. Nor can I imagine getting my mind around the notion that God allowed this to happen. Still less that God might have sacrificed my child's well-being because he had some greater goods in view down the road.

What kind of greater goods might those be anyway? Consider one disturbing providential possibility. Could it be that God allowed O'Grady to rape Ann because God knew that this would bring about conditions that would ultimately lead to O'Grady's later redemption and his reconciliation with his many victims, including Ann and her parents, in heaven? On this hypothetical scenario, Ann becomes a sort of sacrifice to provide the occasion for O'Grady's redemption. Perhaps that is a noble notion in which God acts to redeem the most horrible situation. And isn't it better that Ann's

23. The literature on theodicy (explanations of why God allows evil) is vast. One of the most powerful treatments of the problem in recent years comes from Christian philosopher Eleonore Stump with her book *Wandering in Darkness*. It is a sprawling book with an argument of both analytic and literary sophistication, and it rewards careful reading.

24. I discuss this case in *Finding God in the Shack*, 115–16.

rape occurred for some greater good rather than for none at all? You might think so. But then Ivan's voice cuts in with a piercing cry of moral indignation: "I do not want a mother to embrace the torturer who had her child torn to pieces by his dogs! She has no right to forgive him!"[25] I may not agree with Ivan, but I get where he's coming from. I understand what he is saying. I can grasp his heart's cry. And thus, I simply cannot dismiss the fury of atheists like Ivan merely as sinful rebellion.

All this horror leaves me with some big questions. If I found myself in Bob Jyono's horrible position, would I join him (and Ivan) by turning in my ticket? Or, like the rabbi that I cited above, would I fumble with it, while crying out how anybody could believe in this God of mercy? Or would I march on in awe-inspiring and unshakeable faith with nary a stumble? I don't know, not least because I can't imagine the pain, the agony, the guilt, and the rage that a parent like Bob Jyono would experience. I have never walked in his shoes, and God knows I hope I never do.

While I can't begin to imagine what it would be like to experience the pain, agony, guilt, and rage of Bob Jyono, I believe that God does. And if he knows that, he also knows the agonizing forces that would lead a man to turn in his ticket. Maybe in the midst of that knowledge, grace and hope can, as yet, shine through.

25. Dostoyevsky, *The Brothers Karamazov*, 287.

6

The atheist as neighbor

A few years ago the atheist philosopher Walter Sinnott-Armstrong participated in some public debates on the existence of God with renowned Christian apologist William Lane Craig. Subsequently the two philosophers co-published a book in which they carried on the debate. To promote that book, Sinnott-Armstrong wrote a short article that appeared in the alumni magazine for Dartmouth College. He recalls:

> I knew that Dartmouth alumni included many religious fanatics. I expected many negative reactions. I got them. My favorite (because it was so amusing) was an e-mail that called me a "small minded" "egoist," "an arrogant fool," and a "pompous PhD," then added "it is pathetic that the College allows you in a classroom," and "That you don't [believe in God], I am sorry to have to inform you, calls into question your intelligence."[1]

Arguably the most bizarre aspect of the letter came at the end: after concluding his litany of insults, the letter writer stated that he was waiting to hear back from Sinnott-Armstrong so they could continue the discussion. Sinnott-Armstrong recalls his bemusement at this presumption: "Did he really think I wanted to have a dialogue with someone who would say such things about me in response to a short opinion piece?"[2]

---

1. Sinnott-Armstrong, "Overcoming Christianity," in Antony, *Philosophers without Gods*, 77.

2. Williamson and Yancey, *There is No God*, 77.

I can sympathize. It is no fun dealing with obnoxious, combative and presumptuous people (Christians or otherwise). At the same time, my sympathy begins to dissipate a bit as Sinnott-Armstrong goes on to speculate that this particular exchange is reflective of a "larger problem" with theists generally. He opines, "Many theists feel perfectly justified in abusing atheists. I would never consider writing such a diatribe against a theist who argued for belief in God. I would remain calm even if a theist misrepresented atheism. Most atheists I know let ridiculous religious views go unchallenged."[3] While I was initially in some sympathy with Sinnott-Armstrong, he loses me when he suggests that atheists are on the whole better behaved than theists (or Christians). While I readily concede that there is no shortage of abrasive, combative, and obnoxious theists (or Christians), in my experience there is also no shortage of abrasive, combative, and obnoxious atheists. And I don't see much value in attempting to establish that one of these two groups tends to be better behaved than the other.

As an aside, I think it is worth pointing out that Sinnott-Armstrong himself does not appear to be above reproach, at least judging from the way he recounts the events. For starters, note that he refers to religiously devout graduates of Dartmouth College as "religious fanatics." I doubt that Dartmouth, an elite Ivy League school, produces many graduates who are "fanatics" of any sort. And that leaves one with the impression that Sinnott-Armstrong has opted for a very uncharitable way to refer to religious people. In short, it does not seem very charitable to dismiss the deep convictions of very large and well established belief communities as "ridiculous." The condescending tone of this phrasing leaves me wondering whether Sinnott-Armstrong is really as generous and non-combative as he seems to think. I'd certainly be put out if I discovered that I was being written off as a "fanatic" with "ridiculous" beliefs. I bet Sinnott-Armstrong would as well.

Before moving on, let me add a personal note. I'm not intending to single out Sinnott-Armstrong here, for too often I find myself failing to achieve a detached and generous demeanor when interacting with others. Indeed, I suspect we're all tempted from time to time to write off those with whom we disagree as ridiculous fanatics. So rather than point an accusing finger at Sinnott-Armstrong, we should all reflect on the extent to which we are prone to treat others uncharitably. (With that in mind, before you

---

3. Ibid., 77–78.

continue reading, let's all take a moment to reflect with great solemnity on our past failures. We're all in this together.)

Now that we're clear we're all in the same boat, let's get back to the main point. I noted that in my experience I have found there to be no shortage of abrasive, combative, and obnoxious atheists. Like I said, I'm not claiming atheists are on the whole any worse behaved than Christians, but I certainly don't see evidence that they're generally better, either. Williamson and Yancey's sociological study of atheists in America provides some concrete evidence of the hostility that atheists often have toward Christians and others of religious faith. Their research began with an online survey of religious belief that they distributed to various atheistic, secular, and anti-religious groups. Williamson and Yancey note that these survey respondents reflected a high degree of hostility toward religion and evangelical Christianity in particular: "A vast majority of the responses were dismissive of religions in general, and most were insulting and derisive of evangelical Christianity. Criticism ranged from labeling the religious as delusional to labeling them as sexist, anti-scientific, or abusive."[4] Williamson and Yancey followed up the initial surveys with in-depth, face-to-face interviews of a number of atheists. While they observed that the vituperative was notably dialed down in the personal interviews, they still concluded that overall many atheists are deeply hostile toward the religious: "At their harshest, atheists may dehumanize those who are religious or consider them throwbacks to earlier evolutionary cousins of humans. Particularly in the online survey, atheists commonly referred to those who are religious as developmentally impaired, brutish, or unevolved."[5] At this point I think we have enough data to justify the conclusion that some Christians aren't nice to atheists, and some atheists aren't nice to Christians. So what say we all make an effort to be nicer?

Fair enough, except for one thing: I think Christians need to take ownership of the degree to which their own widespread and centuries-old prejudices toward atheists might have precipitated (or at least spurred on) this whole lamentable cycle of escalating hostilities. At this point we can make an appeal to Newton's Third Law: For every action, there is an equal and opposite reaction. Given the fact that Christians have long marginalized atheists by tarring them with the brush of the Rebellion Thesis, is it any surprise that many atheists have responded in kind? So while we may

4. Ibid., 14.
5. Ibid., 15.

all presently be caught in a vicious cycle of hostility, Christians should recognize our role in starting the cycle as well as the extent to which we are responsible to heal it.

So all you Christians out there, I'm talking to you. The ball's in our court. How can we begin to heal this deep rift? The good news is that the answer isn't that complicated (although that doesn't mean it is easy). Here it is: *we must rediscover true hospitality*. And the place to start is by emptying your cup.

From hostility to hospitality

The great Catholic spirituality writer Henri Nouwen tells the story of a Zen master who agreed to meet with a university professor. After the professor was seated, the Zen master placed a teacup on the table and began pouring the steaming liquid into the cup. And he kept pouring even as the tea overflowed the lip of the cup and splashed onto the table. The professor couldn't help but interject: "It is overfull. No more will go in!" The master then stopped pouring, looked at the professor, and observed, "You are full of your opinions and speculations. How can I show you Zen unless you first empty your cup?"[6]

Nouwen tells this story to convey a lesson about hospitality. The cup is a metaphor for our understanding of ourselves, others, and the world around us. All too often when we interact with others, our cups are already full of various prior assumptions, prejudices, and the like. When this happens there is no room to receive or learn from others. If we really are interested in learning from others, and thereby overcoming the endless cycle of escalating hostilities, we must first empty our cups.

A few years ago a lady I know (I'll call her Jan) was working as a chaplain at a large hospital. While she labored alongside people from many different faith traditions—Jewish, Muslim, Buddhist—during one coffee break she told the other chaplains that she could not work with a Wiccan. Unbeknownst to her, one of the other chaplains sitting at the table was herself a Wiccan. (Oops.) At the end of the day Jan was called into her supervisor and reprimanded.

Now Jan was coming to me (the trusty seminary professor) to ask my opinion. I could see that she was frustrated and offended that this Wiccan had taken action against her and she wanted redress. It soon became

6. Nouwen, *Reaching Out*, 76.

evident that my response was not what she had hoped . . . or expected. This was my first question to her: "Do you know what Wiccans believe?" She looked puzzled and then reiterated, "Well she's a *witch*," as if I had missed that detail in her first telling of the story. "Yes," I replied, "But do you know what she, as a Wiccan, *believes*? Have you looked at the Wiccan pantheistic concept of God? Are you familiar with Wiccan ethics? Have you ever talked to her to understand her perspective?"

When I posed those questions I was inviting Jan to empty her cup. It was clear that she had all sorts of assumptions about Wiccans drawn from pop-cultural depictions ranging from the old sitcom *Bewitched* to popular Hollywood movies like *The Witches of Eastwick*, and of course the iconic images that come with every Halloween (black cats, cauldrons, brooms, etc.). But if she wanted to reevaluate her summary dismissal of Wiccans in her original comment, she first needed to empty her cup and discover what it is that Wiccans really believe and how they seek to live. Had she done this, I believe she might well have come to reevaluate her initial objection to working with Wiccans.

Just as Jan had her cup filled with misconceptions about Wicca, so Christians and atheists often have their cups filled with misconceptions of the other. Atheists may assume that the Christians are fanatics, or that they're fearful of life without God, or that they're especially irrational and credulous, and that being Christian includes a long list of additional commitments. For example, it is not uncommon to find atheists assuming that Christianity commits one to being pro-capitalism, anti-woman, pro-gun, anti-environment, pro-war, anti-immigrant, and so on. (I envision Jesus doing a face-palm when he reads that list.) If atheists really want to understand Christians in all their diversity, the first thing I would suggest is that they empty their cups of these kinds of assumptions. Make an effort to get to know some Christians from diverse cultural, ecclesial, and socio-economic backgrounds and then seek to understand what they believe and why. Incidentally, I recognize that many atheists come from Christian backgrounds. And as a result, they might assume that this step is unnecessary: in short, been there, done that. To those atheists I say, please don't summarily judge (and dismiss) all Christians based on your experience of Christianity, no matter how bad it may have been. If the only Christians you've met preach six-day creationism and deny global warming (for example), then you need to meet more Christians.

As for my fellow Christians, this entire book has been a call for them to empty the noxious brew that so often fills their cups. The Rebellion Thesis has prejudiced countless conversations and poisoned innumerable relationships. It has bred suspicion, condescension, and hostility. The time is long overdue for Christians to empty that cup and get to know atheists as individuals. Admittedly, that could be a daunting journey and when faced with uncertain terrain, a guide is always a good idea. With that in mind, I'd like to suggest that we get some tips from our good friend, Pope Francis.

The Pope and the Atheist

When Jorge Mario Bergoglio became pope, he surprised and delighted the world by choosing the name Francis, a clear nod back to the beloved medieval saint. Everybody knows that famous saying from St. Francis: "Preach the gospel always, and if necessary use words." Truth be known, there is no evidence that Francis ever uttered that sentence. But it hardly matters, for the phrase powerfully captures the spirit of his entire life. Indeed there is a delightful irony in the fact that Francis *didn't* say the words, for his life and actions spoke them loud and clear. So when Jorge Mario Bergoglio became Pope Francis he was signaling to the world the kind of pope he'd be, namely one who led with his actions.

He has not disappointed.

My favorite "Francis moment," and the one most relevant to the current discussion, came in 2013. The stage was set when Pope Francis raised eyebrows around the world with his Wednesday morning homily of May 22. The Pope began: "The Lord has redeemed all of us, all of us, with the Blood of Christ: all of us, not just Catholics. Everyone! 'Father, the atheists?' Even the atheists. Everyone!"[7]

You can bet *that* caused a stir. Atheists? Aren't those the people who *hate God* and *stubbornly refuse to acknowledge his existence?* What is the head of Christendom doing giving *godless atheists* a favorable mention? And he wasn't even finished. Moments later in the homily the Pope returned to hammer some more on the theme: "We must meet one another doing good. 'But I don't believe, Father, I am an atheist!' But do good: we will meet one another there."[8]

7. Kokx, "What Pope Francis Really Said about Atheists."
8. Ibid.

Atheists being redeemed? Atheists doing good? Just what was Pope Francis thinking?

It should be no surprise that these unexpected comments spurred on a flurry of controversy. As is so often the case in matters of religion, several news agencies offered clumsy summaries that hopelessly garbled the story. In particular, many errantly concluded the Pope was teaching atheists go to heaven by good works. (Jesus is doing another face palm with that one.) Needless to say, the Pope certainly *wasn't* saying that. He was simply showing the possibilities that are opened up when you empty your cup of the noxious Rebellion Thesis. And by doing that he was extending a welcome to all people to join in works of the kingdom, regardless of whether they are as yet ready to acknowledge the King. To be honest, I don't see that Pope Francis was being any more radical here than Jesus was two millennia ago when he placed a Samaritan at the center of his parable of kingdom work. Of course, being no more radical than Jesus isn't too bad given that Jesus turned the world upside down!

That address was a memorable moment, and it set the stage for my personal favorite Pope Francis moment. A week after Pope Francis made these surprisingly conciliatory comments, he met with José Mujica, the president of Uruguay. To be sure, Francis meets with heads of state regularly, but this was noteworthy since Mujica was an avowed atheist. And yet, when they met at the Vatican, they embraced warmly and Mujica delightedly referred to the smiling pontiff as a "friendly neighbor." And so began a lively and surprisingly warm discussion, and a most unlikely friendship.[9]

After the meeting the Holy See reported, "The Pope is very pleased for having met with a wise man."[10] The reference to Mujica as a wise man was not mere diplomatic speak; it was a shot across the bow of every cursory dismissal of atheists as fools. Once you've emptied your cup you can come to recognize how many atheists are thoughtful, kind, and reflective people. And with that you are ready to receive the wisdom and insight they have to offer, even as you share your own.

At first blush, you'd assume that a pope and an atheist wouldn't have much in common. However, Pope Francis and President Mujica have some significant common ground, and I'm not simply referring to their shared Latin American origins. They also share a beautiful commitment to

9. "Francis and Mujica Full of Praise for Each Other Share 45 Minutes in the Vatican."

10. Ibid.

humble, simple living. To begin with, consider Pope Francis. In contrast to the pomp of so many popes in history, Francis has made it a hallmark of his pontificate to follow Jesus Christ in humility. And like his name source St. Francis, he has lived this goal out in his actions, including the time he washed the feet of a jailed Muslim woman, or the time he embraced and blessed a man covered with tumors, or the time he shared his birthday breakfast with three homeless people. I could go on, but suffice it to say that I have learned much from Pope Francis, all the more as I see the contrast he presents with the many regal popes of history decked out in their bejeweled papal tiaras, luxuriant robes, and gold rings.

Next up, consider President Mujica. Like the wealthiest popes, presidents have long been known for their high living, but not Mujica. Although he is Uruguay's head of state, he chooses to live in a humble shack with a loving three-legged dog and a sputtering old Volkswagen Beetle. And if that were not humble enough, Mujica donates 90 percent of his salary to charity. In an interview with the BBC he addressed the world media's declaration that he is the "World's Poorest President" with a delightful inversion: "They say I am the poor president. No, I am not a poor president. Poor people are those who always want more and more, those who never have enough of anything. Those are the poor because they are in a never-ending cycle and they won't ever have enough time in their lives."[11] Wow, when the papacy called Mujica a "wise man" they weren't kidding! Those words sound like they're straight out of the Beatitudes!

In conclusion, Pope Francis and President Mujica may not share a belief in God, but they share much else of great importance. Imagine how tragic it would be if each had missed what the other had to share because their cups were already full.

Learning from your atheist neighbor

It's time to take a closer look at the Christian practice of hospitality that we find in both St. Francis and his papal namesake (and, for that matter, in atheists like Mujica). This understanding of hospitality constituted a quiet revolution in the ancient Greco-Roman world. As Christine Pohl observes, ancient Greeks and Romans understood hospitality in the terms of reciprocal acts of benevolence extended between social equals.[12] In short, it was

11. "Uruguay's Jose Mujica."
12. Pohl, *Making Room*, 18.

the *quid pro quo:* you rub my back and I'll rub yours. The Christians broke from this tradition by reconfiguring hospitality as a welcome that one extends toward the stranger purely out of care for the other *regardless of any perceived practical or social benefit.*[13] The fourth-century pagan Emperor Julian "the Apostate" may have dismissed Christianity as a form of atheism, but he couldn't deny the fact that radical acts of hospitality were fueling the growth of the church: "Why do we not observe that it is their benevolence to strangers, their care for the graves of the dead, and the pretended holiness of their lives that have done most to increase atheism [i.e., Christianity]?"[14]

So what would this radical kind of hospitality look like in our day? Well, when we're talking about strangers who are often not extended hospitality, the atheist certainly qualifies. As we have seen, discrimination against atheism continues to be widespread. To make matters worse, atheists have often been derided as "anti-American" and "communist."[15] Set against this backdrop, it becomes all the more important for Christians to stand with atheists as individuals and communities, to become attuned to their concerns, to seek mutual understanding, and to create that space of hospitality in which all this can occur.

That said, we should also be prepared for the fact that reaching out to the "stranger" who is so often misunderstood, ignored, and/or marginalized may be perceived as a provocative, destabilizing act. Christian hospitality requires not merely courtesy, but also courage. We're not simply talking about a socially innocuous act like an invitation to have familiar friends and neighbors over for dinner. We're talking about reaching out and creating comfortable space for those who are often marginalized as outsiders. And that can indeed be perceived as a radical act, one that shakes up the status quo. As Pohl observes, "Although we often think of hospitality as a tame and pleasant practice, Christian hospitality has always had a subversive, countercultural dimension."[16]

In her book *Making Room* Pohl goes on to unpack the subversive power of hospitality. She writes:

> Because the practice of hospitality is so significant in establishing and reinforcing social relationships and moral bonds, we notice its more subversive character only when socially undervalued

13. Ibid., 21.
14. Cited in ibid., 44.
15. Williamson and Yancey, *There is No God*, 27.
16. Pohl, *Making Room*, 61.

persons are welcomed. In contrast to a more tame hospitality that welcomes persons already well situated in a community, hospitality that welcomes "the least" and recognizes their equal value can be an act of resistance and defiance, a challenge to the values and expectations of the larger community.

People view hospitality as quaint and tame partly because they do not understand the power of recognition.[17]

I especially appreciate Pohl's highlighting "the power of recognition," because there is indeed great power in recognizing, and thus making space for, the other. When Christians extend hospitality to the atheist, they are reaching out not merely to a stranger, but to a person who may have suffered much for their convictions, and who could have many insights to share from their experiences.[18]

Practical steps forward

So here's a practical question. How can Christians (individuals and churches) begin to extend hospitality to their atheist neighbors? Let's start with the basics. When you hear Christians making prejudicial comments against atheists, challenge them on it. Don't let pastors get away with criticizing atheists from the pulpit. Most definitely don't let them get away with declaring atheists brain dead. And if you ever hear a rendition of the "Atheist day" joke, speak up, tell people it isn't funny, and tell them why. (Also tell them it's not true, in case they think otherwise.) And be prepared for the fact that even modest actions like these can be seen as an affront. However, this destabilization is necessary if we're going to create the space for true hospitality.

This brings me to the second step. Invest some time learning about the views of individual atheists. In recent years, many books have been published which present atheist views. In particular, I would recommend two books: Louise Antony's edited volume *Philosophers without Gods: Meditations on Atheism and the Secular Life* and Russell Blackford and Udo Schüklenk's edited volume *50 Voices of Disbelief: Why We Are Atheists.* The value of these two books is that they gather together the opinions of many different atheists. And that is a great way to begin to acquaint oneself with the diversity of opinion within this belief community.

17. Ibid., 62.

18. On this point I heartily recommend Merold Westphal's book *Suspicion and Faith.*

The last decade has seen a flurry of other volumes written by individual atheists, often including both arguments and some "spiritual-to-secular" autobiography (e.g. a story of how they left Christianity behind). Among the books of this type worth reading I'd recommend John Loftus, *Why I Became an Atheist: A former Preacher Rejects Christianity* and Dan Barker, *Godless: How an Evangelical Preacher Became One of America's Leading Atheists*. Both of these books combine some spiritual-to-secular autobiography along with a raft of arguments (of varying strengths) in support of their deconversions. Also worthwhile is Hemant Mehta's *I Sold My Soul on eBay: Viewing Faith through an Atheist's Eyes*. Mehta's book describes his experiences visiting several Christian churches to discover what Christians believe and how they live. In his foreword to the book, Christian writer and pastor Rob Bell observes, "As you try to figure out what exactly his [Mehta's] agenda is, you'll probably arrive at the same conclusion I did. I think he's simply after the truth."[19] I don't need to tell you that Bell's conclusion runs directly against the Rebellion Thesis.

This brings us to the next step. If you already know some atheists, then you might try having a discussion with them over some of the things you're reading. Along the way find out what they think about God, Christianity, and the Bible. Also don't be surprised if you encounter some initial hostility or derision. A friend of mine used to work in an office with an atheist who loved to challenge Christians on the violence in the Bible. This fellow's trump card, which he seemed to relish, was to refer to Joshua as the "Jewish Hitler." Predictably, my friend and the other Christians in the office did their best to steer clear of him. No surprise there: from what I could see, the man really enjoyed goading the Christians. I understand that it could be intimidating to engage a person like that, and depending on their degree of hostility you may not want to try getting into a discussion. But if you do, remember that simply admitting when the fellow has a point is a great first step toward building a bridge. With that in mind, if I were in that office I would read up on the problem of divine violence in the Bible, both from an atheist's perspective (e.g., Richard Dawkins' discussion in *The God Delusion*) and a Christian perspective (e.g., Eric Seibert's discussion in *The Violence of Scripture*). Simply recognizing the problem and conceding that there are challenges to Christianity could go some distance toward defusing antagonism and providing a new opportunity to cultivate the space for true hospitality and new friendship.

19. Rob Bell, foreword to Mehta, *I Sold My Soul on eBay*, xi.

Next, if you're really courageous, you might want to visit the local chapter of an atheist, humanist, and/or skeptic club. That would be a great way to get to know people. And talk about really stepping out of your comfort zone! Of course, it'd be up to you whether you want to advertise that you're a Christian or whether you'd prefer to go incognito. (But whatever you do, you should probably leave your WWJD? ball cap at home.) One more thing: if you do visit an atheist meeting, be ready to follow the group out afterwards to a coffee shop or pub. I've found that the best (and most honest) conversations tend to happen after the formal agenda is concluded.

Finally, if you *really* want to shake things up, you might consider taking the next step of challenging your church to reach out as a community of faith. Given the number of atheist, humanist, and skeptic clubs across North America today, there may very well be one not far from your church. (This is especially likely if your church is near a university or college.) With that in mind, how about exploring ways that your church can extend hospitality to one of those groups? For example, you could offer free space for their monthly meetings. (Atheist groups usually don't have large budgets.) Wouldn't it be cool to have a group of people, potentially including many who have been alienated by the church, meeting regularly under a church roof? (You could even provide the refreshments during their meetings!)

And how about getting your church to join with an atheist group to work together on a social service project? Despite the many differences between Christians and atheists, there are also significant areas where the two groups can pursue joint ethical action and social change. For starters, you could team up to run a blood drive or build a house for Habitat for Humanity or collect donations for the food bank. It would be great to go door to door collecting canned food under the banner of "The First Baptist Church and American Atheists of Peoria, Illinois." You can bet that that'd turn some heads! (Heck, you might even end up on the cover of the town newspaper!)

Next, you could move from joint ethical and social action to substantive dialogue. And I'm not thinking of the overdone debates about whether God exists. In my experience debates tend to deepen oppositional thinking and triumphalism, rather than cultivating humility and opening up the lines of communication. Instead, I'm thinking of something like a philosopher's café that promises good coffee and open dialogue in a non-threatening environment. And if you still want to do a debate, you might consider mixing up the standard format. A little while ago I was invited by an atheist group to debate an atheist apologist. I replied as follows:

Thanks for the invitation. Unfortunately, I am not interested in a conventional debate format. In my experience it tends to reinforce dogmatic partisanship/tribalism. I would, however, be very interested in a debate format in which I defend atheism and the atheist defends theism. There is nothing better for intellectual nuance and charity than committing oneself to the defense of the opposing side.[20]

Sadly, I didn't hear back from the group. It would seem that they were only interested in the standard "us vs. them" debate. Having participated in several such debates, I'm presently more interested in ways the two sides can learn to say "we." As Nouwen puts it, "Hospitality is not to change people, but to offer them space where change can take place. It is not to bring men and women over to our side, but to offer freedom not disturbed by dividing lines."[21]

Those are just some ideas to get us started. With the Rebellion Thesis behind us we are now on the threshold of an exciting and challenging journey. There are many other big and small ways that you can reach out, overturn prejudice, remake assumptions, seek new understanding, build bridges, extend hospitality, and receive it in kind. So think big and wear a smile, for the time is ripe to step out in order to bless, and be blessed by, the atheist who is your neighbor.

20. For further discussion, see my article "Why Debates on the Existence of God Tend to Do More Harm than Good."

21. Nouwen, *Reaching Out*, 71.

Bibliography

Antony, Louise M., ed. *Philosophers without Gods: Meditations on Atheism and Secular Life*. Oxford: Oxford University Press, 2007.

"Atheism—The Denial of God's Existence." In *Nelson's Quick Reference Topical Bible Index* Nashville, TN: Thomas Nelson, 1995. http://books.google.ca/books?id=H26Ypuskgf gC&q=atheism#v=snippet&q=atheism&f=false

"Atheist Shoe Co.: Postal Service Discriminating against Shipments to Godless Americans (and the Interesting Way They Say They Found Out)." *The Blaze*. Last modified, March 27, 2013. http://www.theblaze.com/stories/2013/03/27/atheist-shoe-company-postal-service-discriminating-against-shipments-to-godless-americans-and-the-interesting-way-they-say-they-found-out/

Baggini, Julian. *Atheism: A Very Short Introduction*. Oxford: Oxford University Press, 2003.

Barker, Dan. *Godless: How an Evangelical Preacher Became one of America's Leading Atheists*. Berkeley, CA: Ulysses, 2008.

Baron-Cohen, Simon. *Mindblindness: An Essay on Autism and Theory of Mind*. Cambridge: MIT, 1995.

———. *The Science of Evil: On Empathy and the Origins of Cruelty*. New York: Basic, 2012.

Barrett, Justin L. *Why Would Anyone Believe in God?* Walnut Creek, CA: AltaMira, 2004.

Berman, David. *A History of Atheism in Britain: From Hobbes to Russell*. London: Routledge, 1988.

Blackford, Russell, and Udo Schüklenk. *50 Great Myths about Atheism*. Malden, MA: Wiley-Blackwell, 2013.

———, eds. *50 Voices of Disbelief: Why We Are Atheists*. Malden, MA: Wiley-Blackwell, 2011.

Borgman, Brian. Review of James Spiegel, *The Making of an Atheist*. TheGospelCoalition. org. Last Modified 2014. Online: http://legacy.thegospelcoalition.org/book-reviews/review/the_making_of_an_atheist

Boyle, Robert. *Boyle on Atheism*. Edited by J. J. MacIntosh. Toronto: University of Toronto Press, 2005.

Brooks, Stephanie. "The Art of the Campaign Gaffe: What We Learn When Candidates Stuff Up." TheConversation.com. Last modified October 15, 2012. Online: http://theconversation.com/the-art-of-the-campaign-gaffe-what-we-learn-when-candidates-stuff-up-9982

Bruce, F. F. *Romans*. The Tyndale New Testament Commentaries. 2nd ed. Grand Rapids: Eerdmans, 1985.

Caldwell-Harris, Catherine, and Patrick McNamara. "Religious Belief Systems of Person with High Functioning Autism." *Proceedings of the 33rd Annual Meeting of the Cognitive Science Society.* (July 20–23, 2011). Online: http://csjarchive.cogsci.rpi. edu/proceedings/2011/papers/0782/paper0782.pdf

Charnock, Stephen. *The Existence and Attributes of God.* Grand Rapids: Baker, 1996.

Comfort, Ray. *God Doesn't Believe in Atheists.* Gainesville, FL: Bridge-Logos, 1993.

———. *You Can Lead an Atheist to Evidence But You Can't Make Him Think.* Los Angeles: WND, 2009.

Comte-Sponville, Andre. *The Little Book of Atheist Spirituality.* New York: Penguin, 2008.

Concise Oxford English Dictionary. 12th ed. Oxford: Oxford University Press, 2011.

Copan, Paul. *That's Just Your Interpretation: Responding to Skeptics Who Challenge Your Faith.* Grand Rapids: Baker, 2001.

Cowan, Steven B., and James S. Spiegel. *The Love of Wisdom: A Christian Introduction to Philosophy.* Nashville: B. & H., 2009.

Craig, William Lane. *A Reasonable Response: Answers to Tough Questions on God, Christianity and the Bible.* Chicago: Moody, 2013.

Dawkins, Richard. *The God Delusion.* Boston: Mariner, 2006.

———. *The Magic of Reality: How We Know What's Real.* New York: Free, 2011.

———. *Unweaving the Rainbow: Science, Delusion, and the Appetite for Wonder.* New York: Houghton Mifflin, 1998.

D'Costa, Gavin. "Towards a Trinitarian Theology of Religions." In *A Universal Faith? Peoples, Cultures, Religions, and the Christ,* edited by Catherine Cornille and Valeer Neckerbrouck, 139–54. Louvain: Peeters, 1992.

DeHaan, Dan. *The God You Can Know.* Chicago: Moody, 1982.

Dostoyevsky, Fyodor. *The Brothers Karamazov.* Translated by David Magarshack. New York: Penguin, 1982.

Draper, Paul. "Evolution and the Problem of Evil." In *Philosophy of Religion: An Anthology,* 3rd ed., edited by Louis Pojman, 219–30. Belmont, CA: Wadsworth, 1997.

———. "God and Evil: A Philosophical Inquiry" (25 pages). Unpublished paper, 2011.

———. "Pain and Pleasure: An Evidential Problem for Theists." *Nous* 23.3 (1989) 331–50.

———. "Seeking But Not Believing: Confessions of a Practicing Agnostic." In *Divine Hiddenness: New Essays,* edited by Daniel Howard-Snyder and Paul Moser, 197–214. Cambridge: Cambridge University Press, 2001.

Dunn, James D. G. *Romans 1–8.* Word Biblical Commentary, vol. 38. Dallas: Word, 1988.

Dwight, Timothy. *Theology: Explained and Defended, in a Series of Sermons,* vol. 1, 10th ed. New Haven: Dwight & Son, 1839. Online: https://play.google.com/books/reader ?id=Kz9WAAAAcAAJ&printsec=frontcover&output=reader&hl=en&pg=GBS.PP3

Dworkin, Ronald. *Religion without God.* Cambridge: Harvard University Press, 2013.

Edwards, Paul. "Atheism." In *The Encyclopedia of Philosophy,* vol. 1, edited by Paul Edwards, 174–89. New York: Macmillan, 1967.

European Commission. "Special Eurobarometer: Social Values, Science and Technology." *Directorate General Press and Communication.* June 2005. Online: http://ec.europa. eu/public_opinion/archives/ebs/ebs_225_report_en.pdf

Exposed Atheists. "Naturalism vs. Theism: Jeffrey Jay Lowder vs. Phil Fernandes." *YouTube* video, 2:07:58. December 2010. Online: https://www.youtube.com/ watch?v=NNSokWhgBIQ

Fee, Gordon D. *The Disease of the Health and Wealth Gospels.* Vancouver, BC: Regent College, 1985.

"Francis and Mujica full of praise for each other share 45 minutes in the Vatican." Merco Press. Last modified June 3, 2013. Online: http://en.mercopress.com/2013/06/03/francis-and-mujica-full-of-praise-for-each-other-share-45-minutes-in-the-vatican

God's Not Dead. Directed by Harold Cronk. Scottsdale, AZ: Pure Flix Entertainment, LLC, 2014.

Groothuis, Douglas. Review of James Spiegel, *The Making of an Atheist*. Online: http://www.denverseminary.edu/article/the-making-of-an-atheist-how-immorality-leads-to-unbelief/

———. "Why Truth Matters Most: An Apologetic for Truth-Seeking in Postmodern Times." *Journal of the Evangelical Theological Society* 47.3 (2004) 441–54.

Harmon, Dan. *Spurgeon: The Prince of Preachers*. Uhrichsville, OH: Barbour, 1997.

Harris, Sam. *Waking Up: A Guide to Spirituality without Religion*. New York: Simon and Schuster, 2014.

Hebbard, Aaron B. *Reading Daniel as a Text in Theological Hermeneutics*. Princeton Theological Monograph Series. Eugene, OR: Pickwick, 2009.

Hitchens, Christopher. *God is not Great: How Religion Poisons Everything*. New York: Twelve, 2007.

———. "The Gospel according to Mel." In *Love, Poverty, and War: Journeys and Essays*, 339–46. New York: Nation, 2004.

Hutson, Matthew. "Does Autism Lead to Atheism? Belief in God Depends on Theory of Mind." *Psychology Today*. Last modified May 30, 2012. Online: http://www.psychologytoday.com/blog/psyched/201205/does-autism-lead-atheism

Jeffrey, Grant R. *The Signature of God: Conclusive Proof that Every Teaching, Every Command, Every Promise in the Bible is True*. Rev. ed. Colorado Springs, CO: Waterbrook, 2010.

Johnson, Samuel. *Johnson's Dictionary*. Boston: Benjamin Perkins, 1828. Online: https://play.google.com/store/books/details?id=nXMwAAAAYAAJ&rdid=book-nXMwAAAAYAAJ&rdot=1

"Judges 5:31." *snopes.com*. Last modified December 1, 2008. Online: http://www.snopes.com/politics/religion/atheist.asp

Kennedy, D. James. *The Presence of a Hidden God*. Colorado Springs, CO: Multnomah, 2008.

Kokx, Stephen. "What Pope Francis Really Said about Atheists." Catholic Vote. Online: www.catholicvote.org/what-pope-francis-really-said-about-atheists/

Lewis, C. S. *The Problem of Pain*. New York: Macmillan, 1962.

Loftus, John. *Why I Became an Atheist: A Former Preacher Rejects Christianity*. Rev ed. Amherst, NY: Prometheus, 2012.

Loftus, John, and Randal Rauser. *God or Godless? One Atheist. One Christian. Twenty Controversial Questions*. Grand Rapids: Baker, 2013.

Lowder, Jeffery Jay. "The Evidential Argument from Physical Minds." *The Secular Outpost* (blog). Last modified June 13, 2012. Online: http://www.patheos.com/blogs/secularoutpost/2012/06/13/the-evidential-argument-from-physical-minds-apm/

Lowder, Jeffery Jay, and Robert M. Price, eds. *The Empty Tomb: Jesus beyond the Grave*. Amherst, NY: Prometheus, 2005.

Margolin, Emma. "Romney's 47% Comment Named Quote of the Year." *MSNBC*. Last modified December 10, 2012. Online: http://www.msnbc.com/hardball/romneys-47-comment-named-quote-the-year

"Martyrdom of Polycarp." In *Documents of the Christian Church*, 3rd ed., edited by Henry Bettenson and Chris Maunder, 9–13. Oxford: Oxford University Press, 2011.

McDowell, Josh. *A Ready Defense: The Best of Josh McDowell*. Edited by Bill Wilson. Nashville, TN: Thomas Nelson, 1993.

Mehta, Hemant. *I Sold My Soul on eBay: Viewing Faith through an Atheist's Eyes*. Colorado Springs, CO: Waterbrook, 2007.

Moreland, J. P., and Klaus Issler. *In Search of a Confident Faith: Overcoming Barriers to Trusting in God*. Downers Grove, IL: IVP, 2008.

Mother Teresa. *Come Be My Light: The Private Writings of the Saint of Calcutta*. Edited by Brian Kolodiejchuk. New York: Doubleday, 2007.

Murray, Michael J., and Jeffrey Schloss, eds. *The Believing Primate: Scientific, Philosophical, and Theological Reflections on the Origin of Religion*. New York: Oxford University Press, 2009.

Nagel, Thomas. *Mind and Cosmos: Why the Materialist, Neo-Darwinian Conception of Nature is Almost Certainly False*. New York: Oxford University Press, 2012.

———. *Mortal Questions*. Cambridge: Cambridge University Press, 1979.

———. *The Last Word*. Oxford: Oxford University Press, 1997.

———. *The View from Nowhere*. Oxford: Oxford University Press, 1986.

Nouwen, Henri J. M. *Reaching Out: The Three Movements of the Spiritual Life*. New York: Doubleday, 1975.

Pereboom, Derk. *Living without Free Will*. Cambridge Studies in Philosophy. Cambridge: Cambridge University Press, 2001.

Pohl, Christine D. *Making Room: Recovering Hospitality as a Christian Tradition*. Grand Rapids: Eerdmans, 1999.

Pojman, Louis P. *Philosophy of Religion*. Mountain View, CA: Mayfield, 2001.

Rankin, David. *Athenagoras: Philosopher and Theologian*. Farnham, UK: Ashgate, 2009.

Rauser, Randal. "Does the US Postal Service Discriminate against Atheists?" The Tentative Apologist (blog). Last modified March 27, 2013. Online: http://randalrauser.com/2013/03/does-the-us-postal-service-discriminate-against-atheists/

———. *Finding God in the Shack*. Colorado Springs, CO: Paternoster, 2009.

———. *The Swedish Atheist, the Scuba Diver, and Other Apologetic Rabbit Trails*. Downer's Grove, IL: IVP, 2012.

———. "Why Debates on the Existence of God Tend to Do More Harm than Good." The Tentative Apologist (blog). Last modified October 4, 2014. Online: http://randalrauser.com/2014/10/why-debates-on-the-existence-of-god-tend-to-do-more-harm-than-good/

———. *You're Not as Crazy as I Think: Dialogue in a World of Loud Voices and Hardened Opinions*. Colorado Springs, CO: Biblica, 2011.

Rhodes, Ron. *Answering the Objections of Atheists, Agnostics, & Skeptics*. Eugene, OR: Harvest House, 2006.

Richardson, Alan, ed. *A Dictionary of Christian Theology*. London: SCM, 1974.

Right Wing Watch. "Atheism has never healed a disease." *YouTube* video, 1:39. November 15, 2013. Online: https://www.youtube.com/watch?v=ugeCQnxsW_4

———. "Hagee Tells Atheists To Leave the Country b/c They Are Not Wanted & Won't Be Missed." *YouTube* video, 1:51. June 5, 2012. Online: https://www.youtube.com/watch?v=75b1FMzGTB8

Sandman, Peter M. "Gay Rights as a Risk Communication Problem." *Risk = Hazard + Outrage: The Peter Sandman Risk Communication Website*. Last modified December 1, 2004. Online: http://www.psandman.com/gst2004.htm

Saunders, Nicholas. *Divine Action and Modern Science*. Cambridge: Cambridge University Press, 2002.

Schellenberg, J. L. *Divine Hiddenness and Human Reason*. Ithaca, NY: Cornell University Press, 1993.

———. *The Wisdom to Doubt: A Justification of Religious Skepticism*. Ithaca, NY: Cornell University Press, 2012.

———. "What Divine Hiddenness Reveals, or How Weak Theistic Evidence is Strong Atheistic Proof." *The Secular Web*. Last modified 2008. *Online*: http://infidels.org/library/modern/john_schellenberg/hidden.html

Seibert, Eric. *The Violence of Scripture: Overcoming the Old Testament's Troubling Legacy*. Minneapolis, MN: Fortress, 2012.

Shellenberger, Susie. *The One Year Devos for Teens*. Colorado Springs, CO: Tyndale Kids, 2003.

Sinnott-Armstrong, Walter. *Morality without God?* Oxford: Oxford University Press, 2009.

Smith, David Livingstone. *Why We Demean, Enslave, and Exterminate Others*. New York: St. Martin's Press, 2011.

Spiegel, James. *The Making of an Atheist: How Immorality Leads to Unbelief*. Chicago: Moody, 2010.

Sproul, R. C. *Essential Truths of the Christian Faith*. Chicago: Tyndale, 1992.

———. *The Righteous Shall Live by Faith: Romans*. Wheaton, IL: Crossway, 2009.

Spurgeon, Charles Haddon. *The Treasury of David: Spurgeon's Classic Work on the Psalms*. Abridged by David O. Fuller. Grand Rapids: Kregel, 1976.

Stump, Eleonore. *Wandering in Darkness: Narrative and the Problem of Suffering*. Oxford: Oxford University Press, 2010.

Swinburne, Richard. *The Existence of God*. 2nd ed. Oxford: Oxford University Press, 2004.

Tooley, Michael. "Dr. Tooley's Opening Statement." *A Classic Debate on the Existence of God*. November 1994. Online: http://www.leaderu.com/offices/billcraig/docs/craig-tooley2.html

Touching the Void. Directed by Kevin Macdonald. 2003. Montreal: Alliance Atlantis, 2004. DVD.

"Uruguay's Jose Mujica: The Poorest President in the World." *Wimp.com* video, 3:48. Online: http://www.wimp.com/poorestpresident/

"Vermin." *Online Etymology Dictionary*. Online: http://www.etymonline.com/index.php?term=vermin

Westphal, Merold. *Suspicion and Faith: The Religious Uses of Modern Atheism*. New York: Fordham University Press, 1998.

Wiedmer, Caroline Alice. *The Claims of Memory: Representations of the Holocaust in Contemporary Germany and France*. Ithaca, NY: Cornell University Press, 1999.

Wiesel, Elie. *Night*. Translated by Marion Wiesel. New York: Hill and Wang, 2006.

Wilken, Robert. *The Christians as the Romans Saw Them*. New Haven: Yale University Press, 2003.

Williamson David A., and George Yancey. *There is No God: Atheists in America*. Lanham, MD: Rowman and Littlefield, 2013.

Zacharias, Ravi. *The Real Face of Atheism*. Grand Rapids: Baker, 2004.

Made in the USA
Lexington, KY
25 January 2016